ROUTLEDGE LIBRARY EDITIONS:
WELFARE AND THE STATE

Volume 8

SELF HELP IN HEALTH AND SOCIAL WELFARE

SELF HELP IN HEALTH AND SOCIAL WELFARE

England and West Germany

Edited by
STEPHEN HUMBLE AND
JUDITH UNELL

Routledge
Taylor & Francis Group

LONDON AND NEW YORK

First published in 1989 by Routledge

This edition first published in 2019
by Routledge
2 Park Square, Milton Park, Abingdon, Oxon OX14 4RN

and by Routledge
711 Third Avenue, New York, NY 10017

Routledge is an imprint of the Taylor & Francis Group, an informa business

© 1989 Routledge

British Library Cataloguing in Publication Data
A catalogue record for this book is available from the British Library

ISBN: 978-1-138-61373-7 (Set)
ISBN: 978-0-429-45813-2 (Set) (ebk)
ISBN: 978-1-138-60730-9 (Volume 8) (hbk)
ISBN: 978-1-138-60732-3 (Volume 8) (pbk)
ISBN: 978-0-429-46722-6 (Volume 8) (ebk)

Publisher's Note
The publisher has gone to great lengths to ensure the quality of this reprint but points out that some imperfections in the original copies may be apparent.

Disclaimer
The publisher has made every effort to trace copyright holders and would welcome correspondence from those they have been unable to trace.

SELF HELP
IN HEALTH AND
SOCIAL WELFARE

England and West Germany

EDITED BY STEPHEN HUMBLE
AND JUDITH UNELL

ROUTLEDGE
London and New York

First published 1989 by Routledge
11 New Fetter Lane, London EC4P 4EE
29 West 35th Street, New York, NY 10001

© 1989 Routledge

Printed and bound in Great Britain by
Billing & Sons Ltd, Worcester

British Library Cataloguing in Publication Data

Self help in health and social welfare :
    England and West Germany.
    1. Great Britain. Self-help groups
    2. West Germany. Self-help groups
    I. Humble, Stephen II. Unell, Judith
    III. Anglo-German Foundation for the Study
    of Industrial Society

361.7

ISBN 0-415-00611-2

CONTENTS

Contents

Contents

CONTRIBUTORS

Dr Branckaerts, Director at the International Information Centre on Self Help and Health

Helmut Breitkopf, Diplom-Soziologe, Volkshochschule, Unna

Astrid Estorff, Director, Kontakt-und-Informationsstelle fur Selbsthilfegruppen, Hamburg

Dr Dieter Grunow, Professor Universitat Duisburg

Dr Stephen Humble, Director, National Association for the Welfare of Children in Hospitals

Jurgen Matzat, Diplom-Psychologe, Psychomatische Klinik, Universitat Giessen

Tina Posner, Research Fellow, Policy Studies Institute

Dr Ann Richardson, Former Senior Research Fellow, Policy Studies Institute, now Independent Researcher

Dr Jill Vincent, Research Fellow, Centre for Research in Social Policy, Loughborough University

Dr Judith Unell, Independent Researcher and Research Associate, Centre for Research in Social Policy, Loughborough University

Judy Wilson, Team Leader, Nottingham Self Help Team

INTRODUCTION

Judith Unell

This book grew out of a series of three meetings between English and German researchers who share a common interest in self help in health care and social welfare. The meetings were sponsored by the Anglo-German Foundation for the Study of Industrial Society and took place at intervals during 1986.

This was not the first encounter between researchers from the two countries. One of the effects of the World Health Organization's policy of promoting self help in health has been to create an international forum for researchers and practitioners working in this field. Several members of our group had already met through WHO European workshops and conferences, and felt that they had gained a great deal from the opportunity to compare and contrast the growth of self help and the problems of engaging in research in this area.

These contacts had perhaps been particularly important for English researchers. Interest in self help as a vital aspect of health care has been slow to develop in this country, both in academic circles and within government. The scene has been altered during the last two years by a modest central government initiative which has made funding available to a series of local support projects and has sponsored a systematic evaluation of the effects of these projects. Research and innovative local practice both helped to stimulate this development but, in general, there have been few opportunities for researchers to consult together about issues relating to self help or to participate in a wider policy debate.

In contrast, large-scale research into self help in health

has taken place at several university centres in Germany, closely linked to the development of professional practice in working with and supporting self help groups. Researchers and practitioners have also worked in partnership to develop a national self helpworkers' forum and a national self help clearing house, anticipating similar structures which have evolved much more recently in England.

It therefore appeared that there was not only a stronger research base in Germany but a more coherent link between research and practice. None the less, researchers in the two countries were addressing a similar range of problems. They were seeking to describe and understand the phenomenon of self help and were debating whether the impact of self help groups could be, or ought to be, measured using research techniques. They were concerned to interpret the growth of self help in two advanced industrialized societies with complex and highly developed health and social welfare systems and resilient voluntary sectors. And they wanted to define the structures that were needed for self help groups to be properly resourced and supported in their local communities and at a national level.

The grant from the Anglo-German Foundation provided an opportunity for English and German researchers to pursue some of these shared concerns in greater depth. During the initial meeting a small number of broad themes were identified, providing a focus for subsequent discussions. Each participant agreed to contribute a paper relevant to one of these themes. Drafts were brought back to the wider group for discussion, and the final papers presented here reflect not only the interests and expertise of each member but the collaborative efforts of the whole group.

The first task was to educate each other about the main features of the health and social welfare structures in England and West Germany. The papers by Jürgen Matzat and Stephen Humble provide an outline of the institutional context of self help.

They also describe the evolution of self help and consider the responses this has evoked in government and in established health and social welfare organizations. It is clear that the growth of self help has largely taken government by surprise and that, although limited resources have been made available in ad hoc, short-term programmes, neither country has developed a consistent national policy towards self help.

Jan Branckaerts and Ann Richardson broaden this

discussion through their account of international initiatives on self help, looking in particular at the role of the European Community and of the World Health Organization in promoting self help in health. They conclude that a policy on self help has proved equally elusive on an international level. Various conferences and initiatives have helped to make self help an increasingly familiar concept and, through the foundation of the International Information Centre on Self Help and Health, have given an impetus to the growth of national and local clearing houses for self help. However, the direct impact on national governments has probably been small.

The rather tentative welcome extended to self help at national and international levels may reflect a generally dismissive attitude towards self help groups on the part of established institutions. Self help is often seen as a fringe activity operating on the margins of mainstream services, a harmless diversion which it is sometimes convenient to acknowledge but which can usually be safely ignored. But it is probably also true that the lack of a consistent response reflects a widespread confusion about the nature of self help. The diversity of the self help group population, the transient and fragile nature of many groups, and the multiplicity of the hopes and aims brought to groups by their individual members make self help fiendishly difficult to pin down and place within a familiar spectrum of health and social welfare services.

The papers by Dieter Grunow, Tina Posner and Jill Vincent explore the problems of understanding what goes on in self help groups and address the question of how to develop realistic and appropriate strategies for evaluating the performance of groups. They argue for clarity about the purposes of evaluation, recognizing that research has often been used to make powerless elements in society more transparent and accessible to intervention by powerful institutions. If research is instead to be a useful resource for strengthening self help, careful thought must be given to developing a methodology which is appropriate to the scale and intimacy of self help groups and which pursues the questions which are important to groups themselves.

Several participants combined a research interest in self help with a more practical involvement in providing locally-based support services for self help groups. Support for self help therefore emerged as an important theme in our discussions, and the contributions by Helmut Breitkopf,

Astrid Estorff and Jürgen Matzat, Judith Unell and Judy Wilson address this issue from a variety of viewpoints. They consider both the functions of specialized self help 'clearing houses' and the possibilities of offering support to self help groups within a variety of other institutional settings.

Throughout our discussions we tried to identify those trends and developments which are most influential in shaping self help in England and West Germany. We offer our ideas about the future of self help in the concluding section. In doing so, we recognize that self help has not developed simply as a response to social and environmental pressures. It has emerged over a similar period in a wide range of countries with very different health and welfare institutions. It has an internal momentum which research has recognized but is still only partially understood.

Part One

NATIONAL STRUCTURES AND POLICIES

Chapter One

SOME REMARKS ON WEST GERMANY'S HEALTH AND WELFARE SYSTEM AND THE POSITION OF SELF HELP

Jürgen Matzat

To understand the development of self help groups one has to be familiar with at least some essential characteristics of the national health and welfare systems. In the case of West Germany these systems are extraordinarily complex and difficult to understand even for most German professionals. It is harder to explain them to foreigners. Therefore the following chapter at best can give very rough ideas about some basic facts; it is a sketch rather than a rich picture.

The health system in West Germany is financially based mainly on statutory health insurance. It affords medical care for the insured and his family, and under certain conditions it provides the patient's income. In 1984 the insurance funds spent more than DM 106 billion; DM 229 billion was the total cost for the health system of West Germany, which equalled 9.5% of GNP.

The cost is provided almost exclusively by contributions half by the insured and half by the employer. Health insurance in West Germany is therefore borne not by the state but by the collective community of those insured and by the employers. Contributions are fixed according to a certain percentage of individual wages (the average today is about 12% of gross earnings).

More than 90% of the total population enjoy the protection of health insurance; the insurance funds do not form a monolithic block; there are more than 1,000 of them such as general local health insurance funds, industrial health insurance funds for larger undertakings, guild health insurance funds for the crafts etc. They are all incorporated under public law, and they have, as voluntary bodies, a board of management and a meeting of members' representatives.

3

What sounds very much like a good opportunity for consumers' participation has become in reality a token. The relationship of every single member with these bodies is characterized by a high degree of alienation and even ignorance. In the last few years the biggest of them all, the general local health insurance funds, started a number of 'health centres', where primarily health promoting, preventive, and rehabilitative approaches (including the support of self help groups) are tried out. If this approach takes off, it surely will gain in importance, especially for groups of chronically ill and handicapped people and of people with so-called risk factors. These new additional activities of health insurance funds are certainly also meant to save money in the long run by preventing unnecessarily excessive use of professional services and pharmaceutical products, and to profit from the positive image that the term 'self help' offers. But they could enhance holistic medicine for the future.

Friend and enemy of this multitude of insurance funds is the highly organized association of private doctors who are approved as health insurance doctors. They provide medical treatment for the insured and their families. The principle is that there should be a free choice of doctor. Treatment costs are settled directly between the doctor and the health insurance fund via the health insurance doctors' association. The cost of medicines is also borne directly by the health insurance fund.

In West Germany ambulatory medical care is provided by a rapidly increasing number of private doctors (83,000 in 1985) who practise their profession 'freely'. For that purpose they need a state appointment. Nearly all of them are health insurance fund doctors. A public health service hardly exists and cannot at all be compared to the British NHS. Any proposals for introducing a public service immediately bring accusations of 'socialization of the health system', which is anathema to many Germans.

Because of their status outside any state system - and because of lots of traditional attitudes of professionals - the overwhelming majority of doctors in West Germany until now have resisted stimulating and supporting the patients, their customers, to form autonomous self help groups. They fear - mostly an irrational fear - the change that the consumers could bring.

Nevertheless, the attitudes and behaviour of doctors in private practice is one of the keys to the future of self help in West Germany, because of their significant position in people's eyes and because of their political influence in our society. And among the officials of the doctors' associations - especially of those in private practice - new thinking gains ground. They call upon their colleagues to start or intensify collaboration with self help groups. This is supposed to foster the doctor/patient relationship, to obtain the patients' compliance with the medical treatment and to complement the widely criticized medical approach with a psychological one, one which more and more patients are seeking via non-medicals like the clinical psychologist, the 'quack' doctors and obscure healers.

The welfare system in West Germany is dominated by two ideologies. The first says that the country is a 'welfare state' and that there is a right to social assistance. Any person who is not in a position to cover his living expenses or cope with personal emergencies on his own, and who does not obtain adequate help from other sources (e.g. his family) should find personal and economic assistance from the state according to his needs. Whenever possible the aim is to encourage the improvement or restoration of individual self help in the sense of responsibility and care for oneself, and thereby reinforcing the individual's rights as a person. The principle of 'aid to self help' is even codified in the 'Bundessozialhilfegesetz' Federal Public Assistance Act.

But 'aid to self-help' is meant exclusively on an individual, not on a collective basis - in spite of the meaning conveyed by 'aid' - there is no automatic support for self help groups. For example, German social work is traditionally individual case work, especially as it is practised in public departments.

The second ideology is the principle of so-called 'Subsidiarität'. This term originating from Catholic social ethics means: what individuals, what smaller institutions (like the family) or associations (like charities and voluntary organizations), or what bodies (like municipalities and churches) can do on their own initiative should not be supplanted by any superior level or by the state. Social problems should only be solved on a higher level of institution (e.g. social services of municipalities, regions, or federal administration) if the lower levels (especially families and relatives) are not capable of coping with them. Extensive privileges of independent welfare organizations from public authorities in providing social services also derive from this principle of 'Subsidiarität'.

5

Most social services may be demanded for free. The cost is provided by public money (taxes) using a variety of channels on local, regional, and federal levels. Additionally special 'welfare moneys' from lotteries, donations, etc., very often collected by public or para-public institutions, contribute to finance actions and services of voluntary and independent welfare organizations.

According to the above mentioned principle of 'Subsidiarität' many means of providing personal social assistance are not organized by public authorities but by independent welfare organizations. As one can easily imagine, this often does not exactly facilitate sensible planning of services. There are six of them:

The German Red Cross (especially nursing, blood donor services, disaster relief, first aid in emergencies and accidents, aid for the handicapped and old people;

German Caritas Association (the Catholic charity network; especially counselling services of various kinds, hospitals and homes, workshops for the handicapped, nursery schools, advice centres for foreigners, training and further training for social workers);

Relief and Nursing Organization of the Protestant Church (counselling and advice centres of various kinds, clubs for the mentally ill, the handicapped or old people, training and further training for social workers);

Central Welfare Office of the Jews in Germany;

Federal Working Men's Welfare Association (traditionally rooted in the workers' movement, especially homes and hostels for the elderly and for the handicapped, geriatric and children's day care centres, counselling and advice centres, meals-on-wheels services);

The German Non-denominational Welfare Association.

This last independent welfare association is in our context of highest interest. It functions as a politically and ideologically neutral umbrella organization for some thousands of legally independent organizations, active in all branches of welfare work on every level (local, regional, federal). A particularly important aspect of this welfare association is its assistance for the numerous so-called citizens' initiatives that have developed in recent years; and the elements of self organization and self help play a much more important role in the German Non-denominational Welfare Association than in the other big independent welfare organizations. Consequently for some time past an increasing number of projects supporting self help groups is based on local offices of this welfare organization.

Although social work underwent a dramatic process of professionalization during the 60s and 70s, volunteers are still to be found under the roof of all the big welfare organizations in West Germany. A survey in 1975 estimated their number at about two million but most likely it has decreased since then. Ten or fifteen years ago a new wave of voluntarism arose, commonly called 'citizens' initiatives'. Very often these people were motivated more in a political way than in the traditional humanitarian or Christian-Samaritan way. And very often they fought for their own rights and interests instead of those of their fellow-men (although they were identical). As mentioned above, the influence of this new voluntarism has entered most clearly into the Non-denominational Welfare Association. Consequently we find here the strongest support for self help groupings, not only for the ones that are regular members of the Association. For example, the non-denominational Welfare Association built up a number of local support centres for self-help initiatives. Next to the big independent welfare organizations the self help associations for the handicapped play an important role on West Germany's social service stage. There are large associations of war and military service victims, handicapped and social insurance pensioners (nearly 2 million members) of the blind, of the deaf etc. Most popular is the 'Aid to Living for the Mentally Handicapped Child' Association, once founded as a local self help group of concerned parents, now well-known nation-wide as a provider of numerous professional institutions, like homes and workshops for the handicapped.

In the umbrella organization 'Federal Working Group Aid for the Handicapped' (founded in 1968) today more than 40 associations for specific chronic illnesses or handicaps are united, representing nearly half a million members, not only sufferers but relatives and friends as well, and some professionals specializing in these fields. This joint association forms a very strong lobby for the total of the handicapped (as each of the member organizations does for its specific illness); it is accepted by governments, authorities, social and health insurance bodies and other organizations for its expertise and as a representative for the interests of handicapped people. The services of the associations for the handicapped include legal advice, information about new developments in medical care etc., very often by means of leaflets and periodicals. Their form of organization looks in most cases very hierarchical; participation of members is reduced to very formal procedures (like elections etc.). Concerning their ideology, most of them stay quite close to the established medical system, stressing their non-conflict relationship to doctors. And they fund traditional medical research programmes. Some of the older and well-established organizations started to found their own institutions (hospitals, homes etc.) and thereby changed their character partly from critical consumers to producers of social and health services.

The existence of autonomous small self help groups on a local basis is still an exception. Mutual aid amongst sufferers is - more or less - a new concept for these big, highly professionalized and bureaucratized organizations, which until now concentrated on fighting for more rights, more money, and more professional services. But new thinking about smaller mutual aid groups has started. Some of them stimulate their local branches to form groups. However, very often these are strictly directed by selected chairpersons, so that participation of the sufferers and realization of mutual aid remains limited.

Another important root for West Germany's self help movement is - of course - the Alcoholics Anonymous tradition and all the self help groups derived from AA. The AA were first imported to Germany by American soldiers after World War II. By 1984 more than 1,500 AA groups existed; plus Al-Anon and Al-Teen groups, Overeaters Anonymous, Gamblers Anonymous etc.

A new type of autonomous self help group operating on a local basis and adhering to the principle of mutual aid ('consumers as producers') occurred in West Germany in the 1970s, adding another flower to the colourful bunch in the self help movement. Very often they are called by the term 'psychosocial' or 'psychologico-therapeutic' self help groups. These groups bring together people who are concerned with a common problem (for example an illness). In regular group sessions over an extended period of time, they attempt - largely without professional helpers and without any interest in economic profit - to change the way in which they deal with their problem and their social environment. The guiding principles are those of equal co-operation and mutual aid. The positive effects of such groups are achieved by the exchange of extremely personal experiences, empathy, solidarity, and social support. The members offer each other a model for (more or less) successfully coping with the common problem.

An example of the awakening public interest in this new type of self help association was a new research project on this topic, started in 1977 at the Clinic for Psychosomatic Medicine and Psychotherapy in the University of Giessen. Like most of the research projects about self help groups in the following decade, it gained a reputation as an enabler of collective self help and it became an important academic ally of the self help movement. Scientific research was at the same time practical support. Consequently, for the federal government who financed these programmes, stimulating research was a form of political action in the field of self help. By constitution the federal government in West Germany has comparatively little competence in health affairs (this is located at regional level), but it has competence in research and in the promotion of new developments by testing experimental models. So there is a possibility of setting new trends. On the other hand, waiting for final results of research projects can be misused as a vain promise and as an excuse for not becoming active. In this way research, instead of offering a solid basis for sensible policy, is in danger of becoming a cheap substitute for it. In the field of self help in West Germany, however, the stimulating effect of researchers cannot be overestimated.

From 1975 on a group of experts and some members of self help groups started to organize themselves, in order to support this new branch of the self help movement. In 1982 this 'Deutsche Arbeitsgemeinschaft Selbsthilfegruppen' (German Association for the Support of Self Help Groups) was formalized as a registered society. Its main purpose was to function as a national clearing-house for self help groups and people interested in them, according to an idea later recommended by the World Health Organization. In particular it is intended to help people in finding the group they want to join, to support people in building up new groups, to advise groups and to bring them together for mutual exchange of their experiences, to encourage and train professionals to co-operate with self help groups; to give information about self help groups to the public, to the media, to policy makers etc; to create a more positive social climate for the groups; to support the establishment of local or regional clearing houses for self help groups; and a lot more. Since 1984 a staff of three full time project

9

workers help with this work from Berlin, where the Department for Health and Social Affairs was ready to finance this project in the context of a broad promotion of self help approaches, volunteer initiatives, and so-called 'alternative projects'.

This Berlin initiative on self help policy at local or regional level expresses the enormous increase in political interest in self help approaches in the Federal Republic of Germany in recent years. Meanwhile a number of municipalities in this country followed the Berlin example by establishing special self help budgets in one way or another. This support on local level, by direct funding of groups and by placing resources centres with rooms, bureau facilities, professional advice etc. at their disposal, will be of the highest importance for the future of self help in West Germany. Here is the best chance to react immediately to the citizens' needs; the groups are really part of the community, within easy reach; direct personal encounter and mutual aid would be enabled. Thereby not only a new approach in community social work will be developed but also an important element of citizens' participation within a community's culture as a whole.

The questions arise: why did the self help movement gain so much ground, why did it attract so much attention in mass media and scientific literature, and why was the idea taken up by politicians with such an enthusiasm?

The crises in and criticisms about the established social system have, of course, been common in West Germany as well as in most of the welfare states of the western world. Some points of criticism which could be mentioned as possible causes in the emergence of the self help movement as well were the unduly strong professionalization, fragmentation, and specialization of institutions and staff members; the bureaucratization and the alienation of the helpers from the clients; the misuse of 'help' as a means of social control; the placing of clients in a position of childlike dependence; the administration of suffering instead of fighting it. At the same time people's needs for services changed: medicine has to cope more and more with chronic diseases that ask for 'caring instead of curing'; between the age groups a dramatic shift towards the elderly is to be observed; new personal attitudes and values of active self-management and self-confidence question the exclusive competence of professionals.

An additional, comparatively new problem was the so-called financial crisis. For a policy of financial cuts the social sector is a relatively 'soft' area. Those who are directly concerned in this sector put up, as a rule, less resistance to cuts than, say, powerful lobbies such as industry, medicine, the army, academic research etc. In this situation the self help ideology was extremely convenient and, after initial hestitation, was taken up with surprising alacrity. Supporting self help groups, it was hoped, would work to enrich the medical and social service system with a psychosocial dimension and - by letting the dissatisfied consumers do this job themselves - to reduce expenditure.

In West Germany today there is almost no politically relevant grouping which does not - with more or less volume - sing the praises of self help or include supportive statements in its manifesto. Conservatives refer to personal responsibility for individual well-being and to traditional Christian charity; Social Democrats reiterate the old principle of solidarity; the Green Party assumes that self help belongs to the same alternative grass-root movement from which the party itself orginates. Only the trade unions remain reserved and suspicious, fearing a loss of jobs in the health and welfare sector. Thus the political parties gave self help ideology prominence in public discussion, something which had before only to some extent been achieved by the patients' own organizations and by academic research. But as soon as unexpected political recognition is gained in this way and financial benefits start to flow, then self help groups are said to be appropriated and instrumentalized, divested of their critical potentiality.

In fact nobody knows how much money actually is invested in the self help sector. The responsibility and competence of different authorities are unclear (for instance because of the administrative division between health and social sectors). Establishing new budgets is a protracted procedure. The federal structure of West Germany (with limited sovereignty of federal bodies) and certain interpretations of the principle of 'Subsidiarität' (that the state or municipality should only become active if independent welfare organizations are not capable of or not interested in solving the problem) make for hesitant policy. Scientific research in self help was a comparatively flexible intervention where a first very limited engagement of the state took place. In contrast to England, comprehensive research projects staffed by teams of academics and lasting over a period of years contributed not only to professional knowledge about self help groups but also to general acceptance of this new concept. Thereby they opened gates for further thinking.

At the same time a large number of regional and local governments, branches of welfare organizations and local health insurance funds put money at the disposal of self help initiatives. There are two main ways of doing this: either by direct financial funding of groups (preferably those who offer services to anybody in need, and who are therefore most easily built into the existing system of public services); or by providing an 'infrastructure' (rooms, bureau facilities, professional advice) for all kinds of groups in so-called 'clearing houses' as recommended by the World Health Organization.

It should be the municipalities' duty to promote self help activities of their citizens, because how people manage their problems in solidarity, how they promote their own health, how they spend their spare time together, how they communicate with one another, and how they help themselves and their fellow men and women is an important part of local culture. The biggest obstacle to further developments here is the increasing shortage of money in the welfare budgets of West German municipalities. This is caused above all by the expanding legion of long-term unemployed people who receive social benefits - expenses that have to be covered by the municipalities.

The consequence of the framework outlined above is that no co-ordinated self help policy is recognized in the Federal Republic until now, whereas a whole lot of limited activities in various fields, institutions, and bodies of social and health care are to be found. But maybe a period of 'let a hundred flowers bloom', a many-coloured variety of ideas and approaches, is much more appropriate to the essential basic concept of the self help group movement itself. From 1985 on the Ministry for Youth, Family, Women and Health Affairs of the Federal Government in Bonn arranged a series of expert hearings in order to gather together the experiences and opinions of scientific researchers, practitioners, and important organizations in the field of self help (and at the same time to respect everybody's interests in a 'pluralistic' society). The result is modest: a new budget of 1.2 million DM in 1987 (the first year of operation) for the 'promotion of central measures and organizations in the field of self help', for the purpose of 'improving the co-operation and the exchange of experiences between self help groups and initiatives', and for 'initiating a network of qualified contact and information centres' (i.e. 'clearing houses'). Sixteen projects all over West Germany are subsidized for three years by this government grant, and the whole programme will be accompanied by scientific research.

At first glance, this project shows some similarity to England's 'Self Help Alliance'. But it must be considered as a very late reaction of the central authorities to a broad development in supporting self help groupings over the last decade rather than as a starting-point, which might be the specific importance of the 'Alliance'. The essential element of the self help support programme of the Federal Government for the future of self help in our country is that it takes up and underlines the central importance of 'infrastructure' (information centres or clearing houses) instead of providing here and there single groups or organizations with minor, often symbolic support without systemic planning. Here government policy in West Germany has lately begun to follow the advice of the association of self help supporters, of researchers and practitioners who worked out this concept of non-directed support in the past decade.

Chapter Two

GOVERNMENT POLICY ON SELF HELP GROUPS IN ENGLAND

Stephen Humble

The subject of self help has come more to the forefront recently in social policy discussion in the United Kingdom in terms of what role self help groups might play in the provision of health and welfare services. The purpose of this paper is to give some background as to why this has happened and how it is happening. To provide that background, some description is required of the health and social services system and the voluntary sector, together with an overview of self help initiatives. It is from a consideration of the statutory health and social services and of the voluntary sector that government has taken a view on self help. It is health, social services and voluntary agencies which are being called upon to liaise with, promote and develop self help groups for the more efficient provision of services. A description of these statutory and voluntary systems also provides a measure against which to judge the extent of self help activity and a gauge of the capacity of these systems to support self help. Readers familiar with the health, social service and voluntary sectors in England are asked to bear with us, but it is important in a comparative study such as this for readers of one country to familiarize themselves with the basic characteristics of the other country's social and welfare set-up.

This paper focuses upon England as opposed to the United Kingdom as a whole since our project participants have first-hand experience of the situation here rather than in the other parts of the UK. There are certain important characteristics of the systems which are unique to each of the four constituent countries of the UK and the English situation will by no means be totally applicable to the other three.

We start with self help since it is the focus of this publication before going on to examine the context in which self help operates.

SELF HELP

Until recently self help group activity has grown without much systematic impetus from government. There is very little literature however explaining why it has grown and mapping its whereabouts. Reference is made in the literature to the growth of extra-familial groups in the industrial revolution, to working class endeavour in Victorian England with the foundation of friendly, co-operative and building societies, to the growth of ethnic based groups in early twentieth century America and to the establishment of alcoholic groups and groups of parents of handicapped children in the 1930s in the USA. There is the claim too in the literature that few groups in England predate the 1960s and that many came into being in the 1970s. Some authors associate the rise in recent years of self help with the 1968 student riots and their aftermath.

There is a larger literature on how self help can solve social problems and how to go about practice in self help than there is a research literature. No one appears to have evidence solid enough to take research samples of self help groups. Studies have been made of prominent national groups and studies of local self help groups are now beginning to appear. The volume of self help activity at the local level must be extensive but it is largely uncharted. Locally funded work in Nottingham and Leicester are probably the best examples of local initiatives and there has been evaluation work conducted in these locations.

Recent national initiatives stand out, of which there are three main ones. Two are independent of government: the National Self Help Support Centre (first funded 1985-86), financed modestly by private trusts to provide support, information and training at a national and local level; and the Self Help Workers Support Network (1984) organized by locally employed development workers for the purposes of meeting and discussing on a regular basis.

The Self Help Alliance, a central government funded programme, in financial terms dwarfs the two independent schemes. As part of its policy on community care, the

Department of Health and Social Security provided £1.6 million over 1985-88 for eighteen projects across England of local support for self help in health and social services.

I shall return to the Alliance programme later in this paper after taking a brief look at the voluntary sector and statutory health and social services.

THE VOLUNTARY SECTOR

In English usage the voluntary sector comprises many different organizations and activities so various that they may best be described negatively - organizations and activities that are non-governmental and non-profit making. They may include paid workers and so are not voluntary in the narrow sense. Paid professionals are concentrated in the national voluntary organizations and in the local infrastructure of intermediary bodies (local umbrella organizations such as councils of voluntary service).

There was and is a large element of self help in the voluntary sector in England. Some of the national voluntary organizations grew from small, local self help beginnings. There is a thin dividing line between what we know as a voluntary organization and a self help group. The voluntary sector can be said to encompass both, though many members of self help groups would want to deny that they were part of anything other than their groups. It is the major employing voluntary organizations which dominate the English voluntary sector and by and large command the attention of central government and local authorities.

In the postwar period the voluntary sector came to play a subservient role to statutory welfare authorities. A resurgence of interest in the voluntary sector came about during the 1970s with the publication of the conclusions of independent review bodies (Aves on volunteers, Wolfenden on voluntary organizations) and the creation of the Voluntary Services Unit in the Home Office. Central government interest in the voluntary sector continues although statutory funding of the voluntary sector is small (estimated currently on an annual basis at £182 million from central government and £351 million from local government, with central government taking an increasing share). However, the impact of funding on voluntary organizations is significant. For example, the funding of Barnardo's (a children's charity) from local authorities increased in the

1969-80 period from 20% of the total income of the charity to about 50%. Paid working in the voluntary sector is undoubtedly expanding. It is estimated that staff of the top two hundred charities are the equivalent in number of staff in private computer services to industry.

Yet although government funding of the voluntary sector has increased it is hardly an indication that the state has been 'rolled back', a favourite claim in Conservative government statements. For example, the proportion of funds allocated the voluntary sector by local authorities is only some 1% of the total local government expenditure. None the less, central government under the Conservatives wants to achieve a more equitable balance between statutory, voluntary and private provision of care ('welfare pluralism' as it is called). National self help initiatives are a small part of the attempt at a better balance.

THE NATIONAL HEALTH SERVICE

Part of the impetus for government interest in self help stems from government alarm over rising costs in the statutory sector, in particular in the National Health Service. This briefest of sketches of the NHS is intended to provide the reader unfamiliar with the NHS, particularly the foreign reader, with an idea of its costs and accountability. I then go on to describe the work of social services departments in England.

The NHS was established in 1948 as part of a much wider comprehensive system of social and welfare services - the welfare state. Table 2.1 indicates that health and social services combined form over 15% of total public expenditure. Table 2.2 shows that health gets by far the lion's share but that personal social services expenditure is much more in the hands of local authorities. Health and social services are a minority spending programme in the total of welfare state expenditure. Expenditure on social security (for the poor, the unemployed, old age pensioners etc.) is well over twice that on health and social services, and there is also additional welfare expenditure to account for in housing, education and so on.

Nevertheless, the NHS is very big business indeed and a central concern of the Conservative government over the past decade has been with reducing expenditure. Since its inception the proportion of the NHS budget in a growing

17

Table 2.1: Public expenditure in cash terms by major programme

	1984-85 £ billion estimated outturn
Defence	17.2
Industry, energy, trade and employment	7.2
Transport	4.8
Housing	3.1
Other environmental services	3.8
Law, order and protective services	5.1
Education and science	13.7
Health and personal social services	15.8
Social Security	37.9
Planning total	128.1

Source: The Government's Expenditure Plans 1985-86 to 1987-88 (Cmnd 9428-1)

national budget has risen from 4% to 5.6%. The NHS, Klein estimates, comprises more than 2,600 hospitals, with 450,000 beds. It is made up of 6 million in-patients and 37 million out-patient attendances. It is a massive employer with 38,000 doctors and 415,000 nurses, 113,000 administrative staff and 211,000 ancillary workers. In addition there are 22,000 general practitioners in the primary care sector.

NHS costs are met mainly out of general taxation, which the present government is keen to reduce, out of national insurance (on a much smaller scale) and out of direct charges for services provided (on a very small scale indeed).

The NHS is a national service, locally administered. The Secretary of State in the Department of Health and Social Security has overall responsibility. The Minister and his DHSS civil servants are able to shape the work of the NHS through financial controls and advisory circulars to the 14 Regional Health Authorities and the bottom tier District Health Authorities (192 in England).

The diagram in Table 2.3 conveys the structure of the NHS. Three features are worth remarking on. First, there have to be joint arrangements between (elected) local authorities and (unelected) health authorities because of the

Table 2.2: Health and Personal Social Services 1984-85

	£ million Capital	Current	Total
HEALTH CAPITAL EXPENDITURE	753		
CURRENT EXPENDITURE (gross) Hospitals & Community Health Service Family Practitioner Services Central health and miscellaneous		9,155 3,368 569	
		13,092	
TOTAL			13,845
PERSONAL SOCIAL SERVICES CAPITAL EXPENDITURE Central Government Services Local Authorities	1 67		
	68		
CURRENT EXPENDITURE (gross)			
Central Government Local Authorities		12 2,672	
		2,685	
TOTAL			2,753
TOTAL HEALTH AND PERSONAL SOCIAL SERVICES CAPITAL CURRENT (gross)	821	15,788	
TOTAL			16,599

Source: The Government's Expenditure Plans 1985-86 to 1987-88 (Cmnd 9428-11)

separate nature of the NHS from local government. Second, general practitioners - family doctors - are not directly

Table 2.3: Structure of the NHS

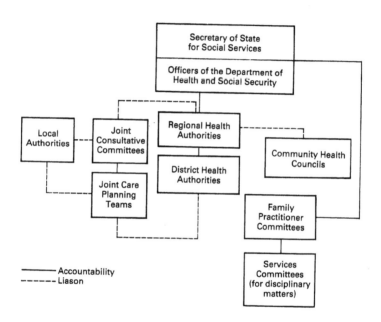

————— Accountability
—————— Liason

employed by the DHSS but contracted through Family Practitioner Committees. This arrangement reflects the independent nature of the medical profession. Third, Community Health Councils are intended to represent the community voice and some of the interests of the consumer of the health service. But they are generally regarded as a token force, without much power and influence.

Above all the NHS is large and intricate. It is dominated by different, sometimes conflicting, professional and union allegiances. It has come under governmental attack for being cumbersome, costly and managerially inefficient. But opinion polls repeatedly show that the NHS still enjoys the public's favour and it is difficult to see how any government could radically transform it. A reorientation of NHS structure and practice is of course possible and government emphasis upon community care, including self help, is part of the present reorientation strategy.

SOCIAL SERVICES DEPARTMENTS

Self help groups operating in the health and social services field are not of course co-terminous with statutory networks such as those of the NHS and local government. But the work of the NHS is likely to overlap with that of self help groups, and so is the work of social services departments. Briefly, the term 'social services' has a wide meaning but generally speaking social services fall into three categories: services carried out by social services departments (SSDs) such as residential care for the elderly, children, the disabled, services for the homeless and deprived; probation and after care for offenders, carried out by probation officers who are attached to the courts, quite separate from SSDs, and responsible to the Home Office; and the work of voluntary agencies. It is SSDs which are focused on here.

SSDs have a shorter history than the health authorities though both have been re-organized in the course of the 1970s. SSDs originated with the Seebohm Report of 1968 which judged that there was inadequate provision, poor co-ordination between local social services and lack of accessibility on the part of the public to them. Integrated SSDs were established in 1970. Unlike health authorities, SSDs are directly accountable to elected local authority councillors. They are part of local government and there are

108 local SSDs in England.

Besides their accountability to locally elected authorities, SSDs derive a good part of their revenue from local taxes in the form of rates. Having this local flavour the Minister in London is less easily able to influence SSD policy than is the case with NHS policy. He has limited powers of inspection and the DHSS emphasis is upon advisory, promotional and developmental work with SSDs. Added to this the personal social services are in a financial sense relatively unimportant to the Minister, only accounting for some 6% of the DHSS budget, whereas the NHS takes 31% and social security some 62% of the DHSS budget.

Yet despite recent reforms involving increased service integration and greater professionalization and despite their relatively low total costs, SSDs have not escaped Ministerial scrutiny. Government policy is to urge SSDs to support care taking place in the community and to do so on an ever tighter budget - local government as a whole has experienced severe retrenchment. SSDs have also had more than their fair share of adverse media attention. There has been a particular failure by SSDs as perceived by the media to cope adequately with cases of child abuse. The media image of SSDs is that they are staffed by 'wet' liberals and there is no evidence of a contrary view amongst the public.

Financial cuts, lack of support generally and increasing demand through such factors as an ageing population and greater unemployment are blamed by SSD professionals for low morale in the service. It is precisely at this difficult juncture that SSDs are being asked to give greater recognition to community care, including self-help.

COMMUNITY CARE AND THE SELF HELP ALLIANCE

Behind government community care policy lies a confusing terminology. Care in the Community generally refers to the government's programme, dating back to the 1960s, to transfer patients with resources from institutions to community care. Community Care generally means care of patients and clients in small units, or their own homes. Helping the Community to Care is the specific government programme, of which self help is a part, to make available £10.5 million in the period 1985-88 through voluntary bodies 'aimed' said the government statement (1) 'particularly at improving care for elderly people and people who are mentally ill or mentally handicapped, by assisting volunteers, families, neighbours and others to care for them more effectively and with greater confidence'.

The £1.6 million Self Help Alliance budget from the total Helping the Community to Care budget is distributed by the DHSS to a set of seven national voluntary bodies for them to decide allocation locally. The majority of schemes are based in local councils of voluntary service though a few unorthodox locations were chosen, including a women's mental health collective and a community bookshop. Establishing a variety of forms of self help is a central objective of the Alliance, and the local projects selected for development include women's self help initiatives, drug abuse groups, depression support groups, ethnic minority self help groups, unemployment groups, self help groups run by elderly people and self help in rural areas.

Broadly, the Alliance operates in eight categories of self help:
- physical conditions (e.g. arthritis, herpes, sickle cell anaemia);
- positive health and well-being (e.g. Well Women's groups, birth information, holistic health);
- mental health (agoraphobia, anxiety and panic);
- life crisis (e.g. postnatal depression, cot deaths, bereavement);
- behavioural disorders (e.g. eating disorders);
- lifestyle and social status issues (e.g. single parenthood, lesbians and homosexuals, sheltered housing for Asian battered wives);
- caring for carers (support for parents of Down's syndrome children, family support for drug users);
- community and welfare activities (e.g. nursery and toddlers groups and ethnic minority groups such as the Gujarati elderly women's group).

The Alliance scheme is experimental and separate DHSS finance has been made available for evaluation. It is not untypical of a recent run of government schemes targeted on the voluntary sector and planted in local areas. It is small-scale and its lines of accountability are obscure. Government wants a different approach to care from the statutory approach but it is hemmed in by bureaucratic and professional inertia and above all by existing financial commitments. For example an ageing population and increased unemployment make relentless demands and have pushed the social security budget upwards. The Self Help Alliance is an example of what government can do at the margins in the hope that by tossing out relatively small sums of money bigger outcomes might emerge.

CONCLUDING REMARKS

This section has tried to convey the political and economic considerations behind government decisions on self help. It is important not to overestimate these decisions. Government has no grand strategy on self help. But given that self help is so very different from what the state sector has so far engaged in we need to know why government has made the decision to fund self help at all. The following points are offered by way of summary, noting those features which can be regarded as important to understanding the context of self help in health and social services in England.

Social security commands the lion's share of public expenditure. Although a long-term reorganization of social security is planned, it is largely fixed-cost based and demand-led - e.g. through the growing number of elderly people and the high proportion of unemployed people.

The 1960s and 1970s are regarded as the period of technocratic and managerial growth in the NHS. Now the emphasis is upon simplification, decentralization and managerial efficiency.

Health expenditure is regarded as in need of containing. A largely free-of-charge health system is still much valued by the public, and hence politicians are apt to hesitate in attacking the health structure directly. But charges of over-professionalization and over-bureaucratization of health meet with public sympathy.

Social services are a considerably smaller system than the health system but SSDs have recently commanded much adverse attention. In the past few years central government and the public have questioned their worthwhileness (though a recent government-backed review concluded that if social services did not exist they would have to be invented).

Both health and social services provide finance for the voluntary sector, including self-help groups, but in small measure. Central government would like to see more expenditure on a mixed economy of welfare, and the Self Help Alliance is an attempt from the centre, aimed at stimulating activity in self help. It is a seedcorn experiment which by-passes health authorities and local government.

Central government has grown increasingly frustrated at its inability to take control of overall local expenditure and is trying to take better control. A mixed economy of welfare is an indirect outcome of central government's expenditure control policy.

Community care, in which self help is included, is the new vogue, even if it goes largely unexplained. Statutory finance, though small, is transforming a historically impoverished voluntary sector. It may transform self help groups too.

NOTE

1. Consumers Association. Patients' Guide to the NHS, 1983.

Part Two

THE INTERNATIONAL CONTEXT

Chapter Three

POLITICS AND POLICIES ON SELF HELP: NOTES ON THE INTERNATIONAL SCENE

Jan Branckaerts and Ann Richardson

This paper identifies and describes a few key milestones in the development of policies on self help at an international level. At its core lies a paradox. Self help groups are essentially a very local activity; they are generated by individuals coming together to help themselves and each other in their own local communities. They neither need, nor are derived from, international (or even national) policies for their development. Yet in the last few years, growing attention has been given, at international as well as national levels, to the formulation of policies on self help. It seems appropriate to take a look at what these are and in what ways they have had any local impact, if not directly on groups then indirectly by affecting the climate in which they operate.

The policies of two international bodies, both operating in Europe, are considered here. These are: (1) the European Community and (2) the World Health Organization, including both its headquarters (world) office and its regional office for Europe. Some comments are then offered on the potential influence of these policies. But it is first useful to set the context, to explore what is meant by a 'policy' on self help and to introduce some political considerations.

POLICIES ON SELF HELP: POLITICS AND PRACTICALITIES

The broad question of what constitutes a 'policy' is a matter of some debate. With respect to any one organization, it is often not at all clear what its policy is on a particular issue

29

or, indeed, whether it has one at all. This very ambiguity is frequently sought by interested parties as a means of retaining some flexibility at the point of policy 'interpretation' and execution. It is clearly convenient to be able to amend many details, perhaps in response to differing local conditions or perhaps according to changed external circumstances at some later date. Indeed, such interpretation may arise in response to changes in the political climate. This is the case whether one is considering a local, national or international organization.

Most commonly, an organization is thought to have a 'policy' when it has formulated - and formally declared - a specific programme on an issue. This is a matter of setting a goal, providing the means of achieving this goal and, perhaps, setting out a timetable for its implementation. Whether established by legislation or simply by administrative decision, a programme provides a formal basis for the assumption of a policy direction. But this is not the only way of judging an organization's policy. A second is what actually happens in practice. A programme, indeed, may not be a very good indicator of how the policy 'works', its day-to-day impact. For a whole host of reasons, the ways in which policies are translated into working arrangements on the ground may substantially affect their nature. Finally, a 'policy' may have little or no practical implications, but simply be a statement of a general disposition in a particular direction. This may or may not be expressed publicly, although it may be widely accepted and virtually 'taken as given' in key circles.

What might an international 'policy' on self help look like? Given the essentially local character of self help groups, the role of an international agency is necessarily peripheral to their development. It is not in a good position to establish new groups, although it can attempt to affect the context in which they operate. This is an area in which policies of 'disposition' might be expected to be most visible. The aim of an international body, in other words, might be to create a climate favourable to the successful functioning of self help groups at local level. It might issue position papers about the importance of groups and the need to encourage and support them. It might also build a concern with self help into policies on other fronts, for instance in programmes for helping particular client groups. The international stance might thus be to focus national attention on this issue.

But on a more practical level there are some actions which can be taken by international agencies to support self help. First, they might set up measures to form links between different countries, to enable them to learn from one another. This might include resources for conferences or other means of information dissemination including an information centre (commonly known as a clearing house). Second, there is the provision of funding for a variety of measures to assist the development of groups, for example, training programmes for professionals on how to work with groups. Finally, international organizations might issue specific recommendations to national governments on measures to support self help.

It is evident that one hindrance to the development of an international policy on self help is the lack of any strong source of pressure for such a policy. Being local - or generally at best national - in orientation, self help groups themselves are not in a good position to make their own voice heard. Indeed, being virtually wholly concerned with their own particular problem or disease, there is little impetus for them to join forces and argue a coherent case. Even the few 'self help' organizations which are international in scope display this same pattern: they support national organizations, campaign on behalf of their particular concern and seek coalitions with relevant professionals, but do not form alliances among themselves. Thus, as described in greater detail below, it has fallen on others to serve as a 'spokesman' for a policy on behalf of self help groups in general. Unusually, this role has been played with particular force by researchers in a number of countries, at both a national and an international level.

THE EUROPEAN COMMUNITY

There are two principal policy-making bodies of the European Community. The Committee of Ministers of the Council of Europe serves as the highest policy-formulating body, providing a forum in which ministers of the member states can meet to discuss subjects under their authority. In 1980, following the advice of a select committee of experts set up some years earlier, this Committee adopted a recommendation to the governments of the member states concerning 'the patient as an active participant in his own treatment'. This had clear relevance to the furtherance of self help.

This recommendation urged governments to set up programmes to stimulate patient participation, preventive care and health promotion. Primary care, it was argued, should be given greater attention and more resources directed to health care programmes which encourage participation by patients. Self help groups were seen to have a key role here, particularly as a vehicle for health education and mutual support. Indeed, it was proposed that recognized groups (or patient associations) should be encouraged and measures to provide financial support to them examined. Training programmes for health professionals were also urged to include attention to these associations. (1)

The second decision-making body of the European Community is the European Parliament, comprising the elected representatives of the member states. While its first two health care programmes (1978, 1980) focused exclusively on high technology in medicine, it has more recently begun to take some interest in primary health care. Some concern has been expressed regarding issues of preventive care and health education. Interest in self help has been limited to specific groups, for instance, the elderly, and often those seen as having particular problems, such as alcoholics or migrants. There is, furthermore, a tendency to regard the WHO recommendations concerning primary health care (see below) as having greater importance for developing countries than European ones.

In 1984, some members of the Commission for the Environment, Health Education and Consumer Protection drew up a resolution asking the European Parliament to elaborate a policy toward self help groups. This resolution, on 'Self Help Groups and Health Care', was to include support for research, support for a European clearing house and the development of pilot projects, especially in southern countries where self help groups are rarer. It was argued that self help groups are an expression of the tendency for people to take greater responsibility for themselves and would save health care resources through better use of services. In the event, the resolution was not passed, having had no background preparation or particular political backing. Interestingly, the vote taken was very close, with only a few more against than in favour of the resolution.

Overall, it cannot be said that there is much interest within the European Community in the particular needs of self help groups. This is partly because attention has been focused primarily on economic issues and partly because there has been an underlying assumption that the private lives of citizens are not a matter for international discussion. There has also been no strong spokesman on behalf of self help groups. None the less, the recommendation of the Council of Ministers proved of some significance in some countries. It helped to provide an impetus to gain more attention to self help, for example facilitating the development of further research. It must also be added that there is currently growing discussion about the potential for creating a greater sense of community at the cultural - as opposed to the economic or political - level. The idea of 'a Europe of the citizens', for instance, easing travel across national boundaries, is under discussion. This may prove the beginning of a new interest in other aspects of the lives of ordinary people.

THE WORLD HEALTH ORGANIZATION (WHO)

The World Health Organization is the office for health of the United Nations. Its Headquarters Office is located in Geneva and it has a Regional Office for Europe, located in Copenhagen. Any discussion of the WHO's policies on self help must begin with its frequently-quoted Declaration of Alma-Ata, including the now famous slogan 'Health for all by the year 2000'. This arose from a conference in 1978, which assigned a key role to primary health care in achieving this goal. The principal significance of this declaration was its shift from a solely medical model of health care to one in which social forces had a role to play. Self help was seen to constitute an important component of primary care. In particular, people were stated to 'have a right and duty to participate individually and collectively in the planning and implementation of their health care'. (2) The declaration was endorsed by the World Health Assembly in 1979 and is the policy of the WHO.

The Headquarters Office first took a specific interest in self help in the late 1970s, via its Division for Mental Health. This appointed a consultant, Dr David Robinson, who had written extensively on this subject, to keep a watching brief on developments. In particular, there was a concern to discover whether it might be possible to transplant successful projects, including certain types of self help groups, from one country to another.

In 1981, Robinson organized a workshop in Leuven and subsequently prepared a paper for the WHO on self help. He argued that self help had become an important component of primary health care. Self help groups were seen to serve a range of functions, not only benefiting members but also identifying needs and developing coping strategies with respect to professional health workers. They were also viewed as key mediating structures, enabling governments to relate to individual communities. Since self help impinged on every aspect of contemporary health, Robinson argued, there was a need for a 'transprogrammatic approach' within the WHO, that is, that every division should take account of it. He furthermore recommended the development of an agreed terminology, the establishment of an information centre in each region to facilitate the exchange of information on research and practice, encouragement of further research on self help and the inclusion of self help in WHO work on psychosocial aspects of health in demonstration areas. (3)

The impact of this exercise was complex. On the negative side, and perhaps counter-intuitively, it provided little impetus to the development of a WHO policy on self help. The argument that self help was so important that all divisions should take some responsibility for it had the effect that no one division did so with any sense of urgency. This meant that there was no one officer (or set of officers) who felt a sense of concern to give particular attention to the subject. Indeed, to some extent, it offered an excuse for no one to feel subject to blame if he or she did not do so. On the positive side, however, the most far-reaching result of the workshop report was probably the appointment of Europe as a 'pilot' region. This enabled the Regional Office to increase its efforts to foster research and to undertake other developmental work on behalf of the self help sector (see below).

It must also be said that there were some serious underlying difficulties in the WHO approach to self help. The idea that 'good projects' could be transplanted to new areas suggests a fundamental misunderstanding of the essentially spontaneous, individual and local character of self help groups. It is likely that the Mental Health Division, itself heavily dominated by psychiatrists with limited interest in lay health care, had little real interest in this subject. Indeed, the appointment of a consultant on this subject may have been seen as a convenient means of appearing to take action, with minimal potential effect on policy. Furthermore, the emphasis given to the 'cultural' benefits of self help by the consultant was not underpinned by a strong concern with practicalities. The recommendations were not primarily directed to securing more resources, financial and other, to facilitate self help groups in practice.

The Regional Office for Europe, in particular the Unit for Health Education headed by Dr Ilona Kickbusch, has taken a more active stance with regard to self help. This has included the sponsorship of a number of international conferences and workshops, the publication of a compilation of papers arising from research and the establishment of an international information centre. These are most usefully discussed in roughly chronological order.

Conferences and workshops have played a regular part in the programme of the European Office. These could be said to have begun with the sponsoring of a conference 'The Role of the Individual in Primary Care' in 1975. Although particularly concerned with the development of self care, this also gave some attention to self help groups. (4) In 1979, the European Office co-sponsored an international conference in Dubrovnic, devoted exclusively to 'self help and mutual aid in contemporary society'. This was the first occasion on which people from all over the world came together to discuss the growing significance of self help. In Europe, it provided an opportunity for researchers to begin to form links to discuss developments. Subsequent meetings were set up, taking place in Vienna (1980), Brussels (1980), Edinburgh (1981) and Hamburg (1981), in some cases organized around conferences of other organizations. These meetings, involving the exchange of ideas and developments among researchers, had a considerable subsequent impact affecting recommendations to their respective national governments, as discussed below.

In 1980, the Regional Office for Europe commissioned a review of existing research and of possible ways of supporting self help in Europe, undertaken by Stephen Hatch. This was intended to provide the basis for an initiative in this field. He again reviewed terminology and considered data on the incidence of groups. Having identified various kinds of support which self help groups might need, he argued for concrete expression of support to self help groups and proposed the establishment of a

European clearing house to this end. (5) At a consultation meeting to discuss the Region's role, it was decided to set up an international clearing house. This was known as the Information Centre on Research into Self Help and Health and was based in Hamburg for the first two years. (6)

The active interest of the European Office in self help did not stop, however, with the establishment of the Information Centre. Indeed, two international workshops were sponsored in Hohr-Grenzhausen, in part viewed as part of the tasks of that Centre. The first, in June 1982, concentrated on the development of support systems or clearing houses and the potential role of governments in creating them. This provided a useful occasion for a discussion of the needs of self help groups for support. The report recommended the WHO to continue to support the exchange of experience, to sponsor research, to urge changes in professional training with respect to self help and to ensure the continuity of the Information Centre. It also suggested that the WHO should urge national governments to develop policies supporting self help, to set up national clearing houses and encourage the formation of regional and local ones, and to ensure representation of self help groups in decision-making as a means of consumer participation in the health care system. (7)

The second workshop, in February 1983, focused on a comparison of the 'services' provided by self help groups and professional workers. Concern with this issue had arisen from the tendency in some countries to question whether self help groups might in some way be substitutable for professional care. It was concluded, however, that such a comparison was not meaningful and attention was again drawn to the need for support systems for self help. In particular, concern was expressed for some evaluation of such support. (8)

Yet another way in which information about self help in Europe has been disseminated is through the publication by the WHO of a book on this subject, 'Self Help and Health in Europe', in 1983^ (9) This provided an overview of the 'self help phenomenon' and considered the perspectives of both professionals and of groups themselves. Contributions stemmed from most of the researchers working in this area, as well as some people active in self help support. No 'overall' view was propounded, but its editors Stephen Hatch and Ilona Kickbusch proposed in a concluding chapter as 'an agenda for the 1980s' the need to 'identify the potentialities and test the achievements both of support centres and of self help itself'. (10)

In 1984, the Information Centre moved to Leuven, Belgium, changing both its name and its focus. It became known as the International Information Centre on Self Help and Health (IIS) and developed a concern to provide a resource not only to researchers but also to people active in the field. Two full-time staff were employed to run the office and it has gained a high international profile. They prepare a quarterly newsletter, sent to roughly 800 people, including government departments, researchers, those running local and national clearing houses and self help groups themselves. The Centre also prepares information packs and bibliographies on self help and answers enquiries from researchers and others. A Directory on support systems for self help has been published. (11) Its Director has taken an active stance in promoting the WHO's interest in self help, for example by giving talks at conferences. (12)

One additional activity of the Information Centre has been taking a lead in the organization of further workshops on self help. Two took place in Leuven. The first, in January 1986, concentrated on support for self help. Since the earlier workshop, there had been substantial developments in a number of countries in the creation of support systems and it seemed appropriate to review their progress. Following a detailed consideration of the needs of self help groups and the nature of support for them, a number of recommendations were put forward. With regard to the WHO itself, these followed the earlier recommendations of the first Hohr-Grenzhausen meeting, suggesting the need to continue to support workshops, urge changes in professional training, sponsor research and ensure the continuity of the International Information Centre.

The workshop also endorsed the WHO's policies on health promotion, with a concern that they encompass self help groups, and it was suggested that the use of information technology in this area should be investigated. With regard to recommendations to national governments, the recommendations of the earlier conference were again supported, concerning the development of policies on self help, support systems for self help and the involvement of self help groups in policy-making. (13) It can be seen that by this is meant that the subject was kept alive on the international agenda, the researchers and practitioners involved aiming to secure the full realization of the earlier recommendations.

The second workshop, in January 1987, focused on the contribution of self help to coping with chronic disease, as demonstrated by research. (14) A number of research projects had been undertaken in different countries and it seemed a good time to try to draw out key conclusions from them. The report from the workshop argued that self help groups had been found to make a valuable contribution not only to their members but also the wider society in which they operate. But it equally noted that self help groups do not function without problems and it would be inappropriate to place too high expectations on them. There are real problems of both differential participation and differential incidence of groups. Some of these problems could be partially overcome with some help.

The workshop recommendations again followed the general line of those of earlier workshops, although some new issues were also stressed. The WHO was urged to give due recognition to the work of self help groups and to undertake and maintain measures to enable them to flourish, for instance supporting the International Information Centre. One new recommendation was a proposal for the establishment of some system for calling attention to examples of good practice, for dissemination from one country to another. In addition, perhaps not surprisingly, the workshop made a strong case for further research in this area.

Responsibility for self help within the European office lies with the Unit for Health Education, in the Division for Health Promotion, along with other issues concerning lay health care. The latter seems to be gaining a high public profile, with the launch of a new journal, 'Health Promotion' and co-sponsorship of the first international conference on health promotion in Ottawa in November 1986. Certainly, the International Information Centre has proved a useful vehicle for the exchange of ideas and for calling attention to the ways in which self help groups can be supported and promoted. Furthermore, there is clear interest in providing opportunities for discussions about self help, among both researchers and practitioners (for instance, those working in clearing houses). Indeed, the impact of these workshops must be seen to lie not only in their particular recommendations but also in the informal contacts they provide for those involved. But the question remains of the extent to which the Regional Office has a 'policy' on self help.

SOME CONCLUDING COMMENTS

It can be seen that neither of the international agencies described has a systematic 'policy' with regard to self help. Instead, there are a range of initiatives and conferences, whose ostensible purpose and effect are somewhat fragmented. On the one hand, it might be argued that these serve to develop a sense of 'activity' among those involved, without threatening existing organizational policies and practices. On the other hand, as has been shown, they can prove to be the impetus for significant new developments, such as the creation of the International Information Centre. It seems reasonable to suggest that they are in a good position to bring together experts to formulate recommendations, based on careful analysis, but commonly lack the backing to put these recommendations into practice.

What can be said is that self help has become an increasingly familiar concept and that some credit for this must be given to the international initiatives described. The same might also be said about support for self help. The focus on clearing houses is perhaps not surprising, as they provide a visible but relatively inexpensive manifestation of support for self help. It is interesting to note, however, that while the European Office of the WHO set up its own information centre, it did not press individual governments to do likewise. Furthermore, there are other policy issues which have not been given much attention, for instance pressing training programmes for professionals to include some attention to self help and self care.

As noted at the outset, the pressures for further attention to self help within international agencies, particularly the WHO, are few. It is not solely that self help groups themselves are not in a good position to argue for more resources for their needs. It is also that the principal influence within such agencies has been medical professionals, often over many years. It could well be argued that the efforts of a few key individuals have been surprisingly successful in penetrating the professional medical Bastille. The combination of the low status attached to lay or community initiatives, together with pressure on resources and concern with issues of higher technology, has put the case for attention to self help in a very weak position. So, too, of course, has its very novelty; unlike conventional medicine, there are no entrenched interests concerned to further its cause.

Interestingly, while the position of 'self help proponents' might be weak on the political level, it is strong on the cultural level. The definition of health by the WHO includes social and psychological well-being. The goal of 'health for all' clearly counts on citizen participation and community involvement, and there is growing recognition of the contribution made by non-governmental organizations to the realization of the goals of the WHO. Since self help groups are concerned with the social and psychological aspects of diseases and with the well-being of their members, since they are a community-based and lay-organized health resource, and since international self help organizations can be seen as non-governmental organizations, it comes as no surprise that lip service is paid to their importance. This high appreciation in cultural terms, however, has not yet been translated into structural change, for instance, positions and money.

What has been the impact of international recommendations, for instance arising from workshop reports, at the national or local level? One is that they have provided an important source of legitimation for new activities springing up at the local level. Thus, the growth of interest in clearing houses in many European countries can be attributed at least in part to the stimulus provided by the WHO workshops. Those involved not only learned about these developments through exchanging experiences but were also able to draw on their discussions when arguing their case back at home. Thus, it could be said that the workshops have been indirectly very influential indeed. This is the case with respect to both the formation of support systems at all and practical means of making them work better. Subsequent research is beginning to show the benefits arising from these clearing houses, both for local groups and for those interested in learning about them. (15)

Any direct impact is more difficult to trace. It cannot be said that international directives play an important part in the thinking of European governments with respect to self help. It is one thing for a group of representatives to draw up some ideas about the role of lay health care, but quite another for individual governments to act expressly on them. Indeed, one might question how far national governments should be expected to respond. Governments need to frame policies in terms of the interests of their own publics and are in any case most likely to be concerned with the electoral consequences of their actions. Thus, governments are most likely to be receptive to new ideas under pressure from their own constituency. This, of course, is not meant to suggest that they do not have good intentions to create policies responsive to the perceived needs of their population.

There is also an interesting question of how international proposals and recommendations on new issues are disseminated. Expressly because they are new, there may be no officials in the respective national governments responsible for them. Thus, it may be just a question of luck if someone - whether a civil servant or a politician - is willing to work on a proposal. If this 'luck' is not there, the recommendation will not be pursued immediately, although someone may, of course, do so subsequently. There are various possible scenarios. One is for officials to begin to take note when surrounding countries pick up a recommendation and construct policies, with a concern in effect to 'keep up with the neighbours'. Another, perhaps more common, is for officials to respond when key citizens or groups, conscious of international developments, begin to question their national governments about a particular recommendation and the follow-up proposed. In this way, international policy-formulating bodies can become allies with local pressure groups and/or local experts in the creation of national policies.

With regard to self help in particular, this is not a live political issue in many countries. There is no broad political base to press for specific policies, although there may be interest in greater facilitation of self care. Self help remains - and probably will remain - a fringe activity, concerning a small proportion of any given population. On the other hand, it tends to be viewed as a generally welcome phenomenon, fitting fairly easily within most political ideologies. Those who seek to extend mutuality and fraternity see it as one expression of these goals; those who seek, in contrast, to extend self reliance and independence also consider it to be an expression of these aims. Thus, while there may be little broad political pressure <u>for</u> self help, there is unlikely to be strong pressure <u>against</u> it.

In any case, as stated at the outset, the growth of self help groups is a largely spontaneous development. This is to say that they are in no way planned by governments, although their existence can be seen in part as a reaction to various statutory arrangements and professional dominance in the health arena. Groups have been started and sustained over time primarily because ordinary people have wanted to form and belong to them. Put the other way around, self help groups are not the direct result of a deliberate 'policy' to create them, at either the national or, much less, international level. From the viewpoint of these groups, the most which can be expected from such policies is the creation of a climate ripe for their development.

It is interesting to call attention here to the unusual role played by researchers in defining the common issues surrounding 'self help' and creating the potential for self help policies, at both international and national levels. Contrary to what a layman might expect, the impact of research on policy tends to be extremely limited. This can be attributed in part to problems of timing, in part to poor communication and in part to the simple fact that there are more powerful pressures on the policy-making process. But in this case, researchers have found themselves in a unique position. Having access to - and understanding of - a wide range of groups, yet loyalty to no one group in particular, they have been in an excellent position to argue the case for self help groups as a general phenomenon.

What researchers have done in practice - and with what motivations - has differed considerably from one country to another. At the time, of course, they often did not see the potential impact of their own intervention. Some created the first directories of groups and set about to bring groups together. Some, stimulated by their discussions in the international workshops, found themselves concerned to discuss new policy prescriptions back home. In some cases, they were notably influential in the establishment of local systems for self help support. Their motivations doubtless varied. Some may have been interested in implementing the results of their own research; others may have hoped for more research arising from a more organized sector. A genuine concern about the social function of research and an idealism to foster what had been judged to be good can be assumed also to have played a part. In any case, the success of researchers in securing attention to self help can be seen to arise in part from their own singular broad view, the lack of competition from others and, it must be added, the receptivity of policy-makers to new initiatives in this area.

This paper has been concerned with the development of international policies on self help. It has been shown that there is no one coherent 'policy' but a series of initiatives and recommendations pursued with varying enthusiasm. In terms of the distinction made at the outset, there are few hard programmes for self help, although the continued support of the International Information Centre by the WHO Regional Office for Europe provides one clear exception. On the other hand, there is a fair degree of support for keeping the subject alive in practice, through workshops and publications. Furthermore, the indirect effect of these activities on local practice could be said to be considerable. Finally, there can be little question that in terms of the disposition of policy-makers, self help has achieved substantial recognition. In sum, while an international 'policy' in this area could be taken much further, it has come a long way in the space of one decade.

NOTES

1.   See Council of Europe, The Patient as an Active Participant in his own Health Care: Final Report, Council of Europe, Strasbourg, 1980.
2.   World Health Organization, Alma-Ata 1978: Primary Health Care: Report of the International Conference, WHO, 1978.
3.   David Robinson, WHO, Self Help and Health, mimeographed, available from WHO Headquarters in Geneva, February 1982.
4.   The report from this conference was subsequently published as Lowell Levin, Al Katz and E. Holst, Self-care: Lay Initiatives in Health, Prodist, New York, 1979.
5.   Stephen Hatch, Supporting Self Help: A Report to the WHO, mimeographed, available from WHO Regional Office for Europe, 1980.
6.   See Self Help and Health: Report on a WHO consultation, Copenhagen, 3-6 December 1980, mimeographed, available from WHO Regional Office for Europe, 1981.
7.   Mutual Aid: from Research to Supportive Policy: Report on a Workshop, Hohr-Grenzhausen, 7-9 June 1982, mimeographed, available from WHO Regional Office for Europe, 1982.
8.   Workshop on Self Help and Professional Care: a

Comparative Approach to Social and Economic Costs in Selected Areas, Hohr-Grenzhausen, Federal Republic of Germany, 23-25 February 1983, mimeographed, available from WHO Regional Office for Europe, 1983.

9.   Stephen Hatch and Ilona Kickbusch, eds, Self Help and Health in Europe, WHO Regional Office for Europe, Copenhagen, 1983.

10.   Stephen Hatch and Ilona Kickbusch, Making a Place for Self Help in Self Help and Health in Europe, ibid, p. 198.

11.   Jan Branckaerts, Peter Gielen and Dina Mulkers, Support Systems for Self Help: A Directory, International Information Centre on Self Help and Health, Leuven, Belgium, 1985.

12.   For further information about the activities of the centre, write to the International Information Centre on Self Help and Health, E. Van Evenstraat 2C, B 3000 Leuven, Belgium.

13.   Supporting Self Help: Report on a Workshop, Leuven, Belgium, 22-24 January 1986, mimeographed, available from the International Information Centre.

14.   Self Help and Chronic Disease: a report from a workshop, Leuven, Belgium, 28-30 January 1987, mimeographed, available from the International Information Centre.

15.   An overview of these research results can be found in the workshop report cited in Note 13.

Part Three

THE EVALUATION OF SELF HELP

INTRODUCTORY NOTE

Jill Vincent

The three papers presented in this section look at the way research into self help can be undertaken. Specifically, they discuss the nature of self help groups and how, and in whose interests, appropriate evaluative research into self help activity in health care can proceed. These discussions are set within broader consideration of the social and political contexts in England and West Germany in which self help group activity has developed. It is recognized that within these contexts certain groups and institutions have the power to set agendas of issues, to frame research 'problems', and to fund - or to refuse to fund - specific research proposals. In talking about research into self help it is recognized that the nature and characteristics of self help groups, their significance for health care and social welfare, and the appropriateness of state intervention and support are all the subject of debate. The terms of these debates are set out in Vincent's paper.

Vincent argues that it is in the nature of social research that no correct position or theory can be adopted; rather there are a number of competing ones. Hence the essentially contested nature of social research. This, along with the uneven access to the power to set agendas and define problems for research, brings the consequence that the interests, problems and goals of the participants in self help activities may not be represented. Thus it is argued that debates about self help cannot be settled simply by an appeal to the empirical data - for instance, the nature of self help or its present or potential contribution cannot be determined in this way. At the same time it is recognized that any position within social and political debate must on the one hand stand up to the challenge of research data, and on the other hand will deploy data in its own defence. Thus research is both necessary and useful, but must be treated with proper scepticism.

Grunow shows that evaluation as a response to the consequences of our actions and the means to considered change is a normal, everyday activity of human beings. Research undertaken by scientific evaluators differs in the transparency of its procedures, the quality and reliability of its observations, and the soundness of interpretation. It is open and available to public scrutiny; it makes self help activity more visible; and it helps clarify standards of good practice. Thus it can be used in support of self help.

Grunow discusses the powerful actors and institutions in West Germany which form the context within which self help has developed. These are the state; the churches and voluntary organizations; the unions and workers' movement, which are the historical antecedents of self help; and, particularly, the medical profession. Each has vested interests - for instance, in cheap alternatives to costly health care and in patient compliance; and each has a power domain - for instance, control of the rules of legally sound practice and proper use of funds, the monopoly of patient treatment and exclusive access to health insurance monies. Paradoxically, then, there is pressure for self help activity to conform to goals and criteria set by actors and institutions against which self help initiatives developed in the first place. Moreover, medical research is dominated by the medical facilities of universities and by illness-related issues: independent sociological research into health-related issues is very low on the agenda and receives little funding.

None the less, Grunow shows that appropriate research has been undertaken: it is small scale, participatory and qualitative; it focuses on processes, goals and outcomes; it uses subjective indicators. It faces the problem that these intensive, qualitative methods tend to give rise to rich but unique case studies from which it is difficult to generalize. At the same time, it generates solid, systematic data which is needed. Participants in self help groups need it because it helps them to describe, review and reflect upon their activities, to clarify their goals, to review possible outcomes and to realistically appraise the potential of self help. Interested outsiders need it to deploy in bargaining processes in a field which is otherwise dominated by medical professionals, the state, and voluntary welfare institutions.

Posner's paper looks closely at the vexed question of the nature of self help. While Vincent observes that self help groups occupy a continuum with traditional service giving at one pole and 'true' self help at the other, and Grunow focuses on the latter, Posner sets out the processes of development and change which give rise to dilemmas and ambiguities. Researchers need a clear delineation of the characteristics of the objects of their research. Hence Posner lists the characteristics identified by Knight and Hayes (1981) as 'pure' self help: groups are voluntary; members share the same problem(s); meetings are held for mutual benefit; the helper/helped role is shared; the group is concerned with constructive action towards shared goals; groups are self-run; groups exist without outside funding.

Posner then argues that becoming successful, expert or powerful can subvert the nature of the group. For instance, success achieved through a charismatic leader may be at the cost of mutuality; and expansion may strengthen pressure group activity but introduce elements of hierarchy and bureaucracy and lessen face-to-face support. Moreover, groups' aims may change over time - a point also made by Grunow. Similarly, expertise can oppose mutuality for it introduces inequalities which militate against the (more or less) spontaneous coming together of non-professional equals which is the essence of self-help.

In talking about 'becoming powerful' Posner takes up the political thrust of self help as personal and community development and a challenge to unequal, dependent and exploitative professional-client relationships. However, insofar as self help remains localized and personalized in its focus it may merely ameliorate immediate problems and divert participants from challenging the socio-political and economic contexts in which problems are structured. These observations return us to the social and political debates with which we started.

In conclusion, and despite the problems set out above, it is possible to make some generalizations about self help. It is a fragile form of care, geographically and socially patchy in those it reaches; some groups conform to the popular image, but many do not; it is at the centre of debates about forms of care and the role of the state in providing them - though these debates have different emphases in England and West Germany; support to self help can subvert its nature and co-opt it in the service of aims defined by others. Its impact is marginal in quantitative terms, but the qualitative gains to members are considerable.

These papers look at the availability of funding, the framing of research questions and the control of research, and the dissemination of findings. The conclusion appears to be that the balance of advantage lies with researchers in Britain. However, the position is changing.

Workers in government-funded research units and independent researchers on individual contracts have always recognized the power of funders to turn down proposals, to delay or under-publicize their reports, and to make some research areas taboo. Recently, control has become more overt on four fronts. First, the department which funds social policy research (DHSS) has introduced a new contract with the warning that from now on it 'may veto any research publication and will also lay claim to all research material'. (1) Second, the DHSS no longer encourages researchers to put up ideas, but commissions what it wants in six key research areas. It increasingly demands narrow, policy-related research which bears on government concerns about cost-effectiveness. Third, government funding to the research councils, whose remit is broad, has been cut back. Fourth, there has been a reduction in the scope and frequency of publication of government statistics.

In general, the possibility of independent and critical analysis of social policy is being eroded.

NOTE

1. Adriana Caudrey, 'Whose Research?' New Society, 1987, Vol. 82, No. 1295.

Chapter Four

THE DEVELOPMENT OF SELF HELP ORGANIZATIONS: DILEMMAS AND AMBIGUITIES

Tina Posner

The focus of this chapter will be the dilemmas and ambiguities which may be involved in the development of self help organizations and the problems these present for analysts and evaluators of self help activity. To begin at the beginning plunges one straight into a quagmire of definitional problems:

What is a self help group? One of the first problems which confronts anyone attempting to study these groups is establishing a workable definition. This is not simply a matter of academic niceties; it affects not only the territory considered relevant but also, by extension, the conclusion arising from its investigation (Richardson and Goodwin, 1983:2).

Who in fact should do the defining? A recent attempt in the Community Health Initiatives Resource Unit (CHIRU) Newsletter (1) to discuss definitions of self help in the context of 'The Community Health Movement' ended by asking, 'Does one person have more authority than anyone else to have their definition classed as "more accurate"?' and then by answering the question with the statement that 'If someone describes a group as a self help group, particularly if they are a member of it, then that is what it must be'. This approach to definition appears opposed to that adopted by Richardson and Goodman (1983). Impatient with more elaborate definitions detailing characteristics not necessarily shared by all candidate groups, these researchers felt the need for a 'simple label'.

51

> For purposes of our analysis, self help groups are
> defined as groups of people who feel they have a
> common problem (typically concerning a medical, social
> or behavioural condition) and have joined together to
> try to do something about it. Whether they in fact have
> a common problem, what they do about it and with
> what results are all issues to which research must be
> addressed (Richardson and Goodwin, 1983:2-3,
> underlining added).

Here, the researcher's definition of the situation (rather
than the self help group member's) is the one which would
seem to count in the end. (2)

Neither of these approaches gives much indication of
the nature of the 'self help' groups. Attempted definition of
the typical characteristics of such groups has been
problematic for social scientists, but it may well be a
matter of very little concern to the members of a particular
group whether that group is 'strictly speaking' a 'self help'
group. Part of the problem is that 'self help' is a 'many
sided, fluid, shifting, developing phenomenon' (Knight and
Hayes, 1981:10; Robinson and Henry, 1977); none the less
some delineation of characteristics is necessary for
analytical and evaluative purposes. Knight and Hayes
(1981:6-7) added to the combined definitions of Katz and
Bender (1976) and Killilea (1976) to produce the following
list of key characteristics of a 'pure "self help" group'; they
are voluntary; members have shared problems; they have
meetings for mutual benefit; the helper/helped role is
shared; the group is concerned with constructive action
towards shared goals; groups are self run; groups exist
without outside funding. This definition, they suggested,
could be used as a model against which actual groups could
be compared. In practice, the development of self help
activity is taking new forms which cut across previously
defined categories and may render such a definition
outmoded. Knight and Hayes (1981:9) recognized this
possibility:

> ... if anything new appears in the world of self help,
> then the original definition will have to be amended. It
> is not in itself a reason for not attempting the
> definition in the first place.

BECOMING SUCCESSFUL

In attempting to evaluate the success of a self help group, should its features be compared with such a delineation as the above definition contains, or should the group's (stated or apparent) aims be compared with its achievements? How is the group to be viewed where successful achievement of one or more of its aims renders it unrecognizable as a self help group according to a standard definition?

Ambiguities may surround the successful development of a self help group. Fulfilling one aim may tend to make success in another sphere of activity more difficult or even result in the group's demise. A group's success in achieving certain goals may depend upon a charismatic leader whose very contribution makes the group's success in terms of mutuality less likely. In a report on The Bridge Project, (3) Ruddock has suggested that 'good leadership' (either individual or collective) is essential in successful self help groups:

> Many of the groups have started because they have one strong personality who provided the group members with the strength to go through the stages of development. These leaders, however, often move on ...

Success in meeting its members' need for mutual support meant that a recently formed group for women with abnormal cervical smears continued to meet for only a few months. Thereafter the women involved, having shared their experiences and expressed solidarity with each other, no longer felt the need to come together. The group's initiators at first interpreted the dwindling numbers as a failure, but later adapted their view of how the initiative should develop, using their positions in a Citizens Advice Bureau to attempt the development of a telephone information and support service. (4)

A group's apparent success and resultant expansion may mean that it can be in a better position to represent successfully the interests of its members to policy makers. A large national pressure group is likely to have more influence and power than a small and local group. However, such success may come at a cost if the expanded organization becomes hierarchical, bureaucratized, and less accessible to its members. There may be a loss of some face to face contact and of the small group forum for emotional support. Such a development may result in different aims being fulfilled by different parts of a self help organization. The National Association for the Welfare of Children in Hospital (NAWCH) could be cited as an example of an expanded group (5) which has, over twenty-five years, achieved considerable success as a pressure group aiming at the implementation of the Platt Report (1959) which recommended that parents should have greater access to their children in hospital. Accumulating relevant experience and information, and itself commissioning research where information is not available, NAWCH is now in a position to be consulted by the medical profession and policy makers. Support for individual parents can still be provided in various forms (e.g. transport) by local groups. As a result of the support, influence and reputation of the national organization, local members may be in a better position to negotiate with local NHS consultants regarding access and facilities for parents.

A group's aims may change over time so that what may count as success at one stage of its development may not do so at another. Both the problem or condition which is the focus of the group, and the members with the problem or condition, will have a 'life cycle'. (6) The members' aims and needs are thus likely to alter as the group continues. Those who at any earlier stage themselves needed help, may become able to help those who have recently joined the group - this has been termed 'serial reciprocity' (Richardson and Goodman, 1983). If the group is to integrate new members successfully, it will have to accommodate quite diverse levels of need for information, support and involvement. Ambiguities and dilemmas also accompany two factors which may promote a group's success in one sense or other - the development of expertise and empowerment.

BECOMING EXPERT

Members of groups may, through accumulated experience or training, acquire a degree of expertise in handling situations involved in self help activity which is a resource for the group, and which the group may need for the realization of some, or all of its goals. But this development can present an immediate dilemma if only some of the group become expert in this way. Then, instead of a group of peers with a common need mutually assisting each other with their problem (Katz and Bender, 1976:9), the situation is again one of 'us' and 'them'. The acquired knowledge sets those members of the group apart from the other members: they become more important, more instrumental in achieving group goals, and an element of hierarchy is introduced.

The essence of the dilemma may be a degree of conflict between the goal of empowering every individual group member and the efficient achievement of some other group goal or goals, such as providing an information and support service. This was the underlying rationale of Cancerlink's format for the development of their local support groups for cancer sufferers. The organization has had a system of 'key members' who are selected and trained by the national organization and continue to be 'supervised' in their local group activity. It was argued (7) that 'not everyone with personal experience has the ability to give support in a productive way to other people going through a similar experience'; there are some people, it was suggested, who might, for instance, use their key member status to be domineering, to boost their own ego at the expense of the development of others in the group, or insist on the rightness of their own views. A need was perceived for a more formal structure than would be provided by a loose collection of spontaneous ad hoc groups, and for guidelines about realistic limits to involvement; however, the importance of having groups of lay people personally affected by cancer, rather than professionals or well-meaning others, was stressed. It was recognized that this combination of features put the groups at the 'traditional service-giving' end of a 'continuum' whose other end is 'true self help' (see Vincent in this publication).

Cancerlink is an example of an organization which has set out to support and guide the self help activity it promotes in a structured way. Outside support for self help initiatives has developed to an extent where it is possible to write off its 'institutionalization'. (8) Those whose job it is to 'support' self help tend to be acutely aware of the dilemmas and ambiguities involved in offering their professional expertise and intervention in the promotion of an activity whose essence they usually consider to be the spontaneous coming together of non-professional equals in order to pool their mutual resources to help themselves and each other. Supporters of self help view their work as 'enabling', 'facilitating', 'resourcing' and 'empowering'.

BECOMING POWERFUL

Where self help is about successfully coping with a condition or problem, changing oneself or the environment, and where this involves becoming more knowledgeable, gaining control over resources or becoming expert, the implication is that the group and its members become more powerful. A number of writers have identified this process as the essential thrust of self help. It has been suggested that the nature of voluntary work has undergone a change, broadening from the tradition of charitable service to others, and that

> the emphasis is shifting much more towards helping people aquire the skills, knowledge and information they need to lead their own lives more effectively and to grasp their own opportunities ... What is happening more and more is that people are becoming involved in working together to improve their own environment and their own community ... this gives the final lie to any remaining cosy assumptions that volunteering is not political. Insofar as it is about <u>change</u>, volunteering has always been political (albeit with a small 'p'). (9)

Such 'empowerment', the essential political thrust of self help which is linked with personal and community development, has implications not only for the nature of voluntary work, but also the professional-client relationship. Self help, it was suggested in an editorial introducing an edition of <u>Social Policy</u> (10) devoted to the subject, is

> a great potential influence on the relations between helper and helped. As professional delivery and control of services has come to reflect and reinforce a service system (and a larger social system) predicated on unequal, dependent, exploitative relations, the self help modality expresses and offers the promise of a quite contrary style of human relations. At root, self help challenges and considerably modifies the traditional professional role ... by empowering the client (it) promises to redesign the professional role and move towards another rebalancing in our human service systems.

In the medical field, the patient is being urged to take

responsibility for her or his own continuing health care, rather than being merely a passive recipient of professional attention when things go wrong. It is recognized that in order to take such responsibility s/he needs adequate information and to be treated as partner. In the controversy over giving patients access to their records, it has been argued that doing so will counteract 'the gross imbalance of power in doctor-patient encounters' and 'help equalize the relationship between client and professional'. (11) Though provision in the UK compares unfavourably with the USA's clearing houses and library networks, there is growing recognition of a need and a desire for more health care information, and recently the College of Health (12) produced a Consumer's Guide to Health Information in which it was stated:

> Whether we are learning more about our own bodies, keeping healthy, coping with illness and disability, or participating in the social and political decisions surrounding our health, access to information is the vital first step.

It is not simply through increased access to information and resources that self help groups may be seen as 'empowering', but also by allowing their members, through mutual support and solidarity, to gain in the confidence that they can change things in their own lives or in their environment. Robinson and Robinson (1979:7-8) write in terms of people regaining control over their destinies - the power to shape their lives:

> It is often said that the natural support systems of our society such as the church, the neighbourhood and the family are in decline. As a result there is a search for community by people who feel helpless or hopeless and without control over their own destiny ... Self help is a natural response to this situation. But self help groups ... are not just huddle-together sessions ... They are much more positive ... self help groups find practical solutions to specific difficulties and provide an opportunity for members to build on the basis of mutual trust and understanding, a new set of relations and even, for some, a new way of life.

The claims made for self help imply that it is a powerful

force for progressive change. Looking at the sociopolitical context in which this force may operate, it is immediately evident that self help is essentially a localized and personalized phenomenon and that its impact is likely to be at the level on which problems are experienced rather than at any level on which they may be structured. Self help groups tend to have limited aims and to be concerned with ameliorating the immediate problems of their members:

> Concentration on individuals and their problems is of course an essential feature of the self help process ... But it means ... that self help groups rarely explicitly focus their attention on any broader structural features of the shared situation in which they find themselves (Robinson and Henry, 1977:126).

The very fact that self help may make a significant difference on the experiential level may undermine the possibility of making an impact on the socio-political level because of 'the danger of diverting from national obligations, of denying the mutuality of class interests, and of subverting dissatisfaction into system-legitimizing do-it-yourself techniques'. (13)

In an evaluative study of the work of Contact a Family (CaF), Hatch and Hinton (1986:87-8) have suggested that 'empowerment' is a term that can mean all things to all men, from an enhanced capacity for individual self help and coping to changing the balance of power in society. CaF is not an organization which is concerned with 'structural change', but empowers individual members, they argue, by 'turning the mothers into participants instead of just recipients' and involving them in a particular form of what Berger and Neuhaus (1977) have called mediating structures: 'those institutions standing between the individual in his private world and the large institutions of public life'. (14) This empowerment results from reducing members' isolation and their becoming part of a supportive network; from their becoming more effective consumers able to exercise their rights to benefits and services; and from their acting collectively as a group able to pursue its own interests and to take initiatives.

In relation to health, Mitchell (1982) has argued that self help was 'seen explicitly as a way of saving money' (see Humble in this publication) and that the move to encourage self help is politically both 'incorrect and dangerous'. By encouraging people to see their problems as their own fault, and the result of their habits, attention is distracted from the social and economic roots of ill health and people's confidence to challenge the societal causes of illness undermined. What is needed, she argues, is 'hard information' (rather than the prescriptions of health educators); acknowledgement of the differences between social classes in their experience of ill health and of lay people's growing interest in taking more control over their own health; and solidarity ('sharing your problems with others can give you the strength to struggle against difficulties in your own life').

The Social Policy editorial (15) referred to earlier acknowledged that self help could be seen as 'politically risky because it hides inadequate investment in social services, distracts from systemic inequalities and shortcomings, and denies wide-scale exploitation and oppression'. By filling gaps in social welfare provision, the danger is that self help 'will simply replace the obligations of service agencies to serve where they now serve inadequately or not at all'.

Ten years later, the first newsletter of the newly-formed National Self Help Support Centre (NSHSC) in the UK is clearly aware of possible criticism of support for self help on such political grounds and defends itself by stating:

> In the current political climate it is all too easy to see self help groups as a cheap alternative to health and social services. It is the NSHSC's role to inform government agencies that this is not the case. Self help groups are complementary to such services and have a very important role to play in advising and encouraging their members to use the services available to them. (16)

At the Third Meeting of the National Self Help Support Network (NSHSN) in the UK (21 March 1986) a workshop had the task of considering definitions of self help and their practical implications. As a focus for the discussion, a list of possible definitions was provided which included the following: 'self help is middle class; self help is revolutionary; self help is playing safe; self help is plugging gaps in the Welfare State; self help can change the world; self help is not a solution to all problems for women'. (17) There was, significantly, both agreement and disagreement amongst the members of the workshop discussion group with all of these statements! These views of self help can be illustrated by the many groups in the health care field who have links with the medical profession which they value and use to their advantage. While many of these groups can be seen as constituting a challenge to the bio-technical emphasis of medicine because of their focus on, and development of, expertise in the other aspects of health care, at the same time they often reinforce societal values by borrowing status from the prestige of the official medical profession. In both these respects they may be contributing to their success.

The fact that self help can be seen in the very different ways contained in the NSHSN workshop definitions is a testament to its variety of forms and ambiguous nature. In becoming successful, expert and powerful (and to be successful in certain respects, groups may need to be expert and/or powerful), the development of self help is surrounded by dilemmas and ambiguities which present problems for analysis and evaluation.

NOTES

1.   Community Health Initiatives Resource Unit Newsletter 4, Autumn 1985, p. 4.

2.   The implication of the Richardson and Goodman definition appears to be that members of the group(s) in question could be mistaken in thinking that they have a common problem and that research can sort out the 'real' nature of the situation. The two approaches relate to different methodological traditions, the first phenomenological and the second, positivist, both possible starting positions for research.

3.   Martin Ruddock, The Bridge Project: An Interim Report, Thamesmead Family Service Unit, March 1985, p. 33, unpublished report.

4.   An abnormal cervical smear is likely to indicate a condition which can be treated and cleared up within a few months. There is no chronic condition to which life-style adaptations might be needed. However, there may be an acute need in the early stages of investigation and treatment for sufficient information and for the reassurance of knowing that there are others with the same condition who have similar reactions.

5.   The original group of parents met on a park bench in South London.
6.   Stephen Hatch personal communication.
7.   Petra Griffiths, Evaluation of Cancerlink's Work with Groups, January 1985, p. 2, unpublished report.
8.   Jan Branckaerts, Peter Gielen and Dina Mulkers, Support Systems for Self Help, A Directory. International Information Centre on Self Help and Health, p. 3.
9.   Liz Burns, Volunteer Development Scotland Annual Conference on 'Challenging the Stereotypes', quoted in Involve, January 1986, No. 48, p. 4.
10.   Social Policy, Sept./Oct., 1976, p. 2.
11.   David Berry, 'Giving Doctor a Taste of His Own Medicine', The Guardian, 19 February 1986, p. 13.
12.   College of Health, Consumers Guide to Health Information, London, 1986, p. 2.
13.   Social Policy, Sept./Oct., 1976, p. 3.
14.   P. Berger and R. Neuhaus, To Empower People: The Role of Mediating Structures in Public Policy, American Enterprise Institute for Public Policy Research, Washington, 1977, p. 2.
15.   Social Policy, Sept./Oct., 1976, pp. 2-3.
16.   MASH Newsletter, Autumn 1986, No. 1, p. 3.
17.   Report of the Third Meeting of the National Self Help Support Network, July 1986, p. 12.

Chapter Five

'I DON'T BELIEVE IN DATA ...'

Jill Vincent

INTRODUCTION

There are some general problems for research into social phenomena which will be explored first as they set the scene for a discussion of the particular problems for research into self help. However, it will be helpful at the outset to clarify the context, meaning and intention of the quotation which is the title of this paper, for this will help to set the agenda of the issues that will be raised. The remark occurred in the context of a discussion about the possibility and the usefulness of evaluating the achievements of self help groups and support agencies. The speaker works in a clearing house. She rejects any approach which merely counts things - how many groups, how many more groups, how many members, how many more members, and so on - without showing how the data fit into a wider understanding of events and relationships or, worse, within an explanatory framework which implies or assumes that 'more equals better'. Moreover, she is defending herself and her work colleagues against those who may not share their values and beliefs, but are powerful enough to impose their definitions and values on them.

Research inevitably brings feelings of trepidation in those who are to be researched. while overt evaluation raises concern that the researchers will be intrusive and judgemental. Such feelings are exacerbated when the interests of those who commission the research and those who are researched do not coincide or are opposed.

We can now turn to the general problems of social research. Fundamentally, these derive from the fact that in social research there is not one correct position, but different understandings or views about society. Such theories or views give rise to different definitions and interpretations of what is going on, see different 'problems', and imply different policy responses. These differences may not be reconcilable. It is clear also that social research is political, for the theoretical positions taken are linked with certain value positions and carry implications for action. This is uncomfortable for researchers and those who are researched as well as those who read and act on the findings.

There is a further dimension to this which has to do with the role of the research foundations and the government departments which directly or indirectly fund research. It is clear that the person or agency which commissions and funds research has, albeit in varying degrees, a powerful voice in setting the framework for it: that is, in determining the wider assumptions and understandings within which it is set, in defining what is to be the object of research and what the 'problem' is. In this way the outcomes of the research and its policy implications are already constrained as they are placed within a particular approach and agenda of issues. When, on the other hand, the researcher frames the research and proposes it to the funding agency, she may have more freedom to set the framework, but the proposal must be relevant within the agenda already set by the agency. Research, then, is rarely if ever free from controls exerted by those who fund it: the question is one of the degree of control exerted.

It follows that it may be difficult for self help groups and their members and support workers to gain representation of their interests, points of view and problems within research, and that research approaches which are inimical to the status quo and whose policy implications bear on fundamental differences of interest among social groups may be silenced.

The role of those who commission or fund research can be illustrated from the author's experience. The research proposal was framed by the researcher and put to the Department of Health and Social Security (DHSS). The researcher has to work in a university or research institute and submit reports but otherwise there is, on the face of it, freedom to operate as she chooses. However, the DHSS fund only those proposals which accord with their current priorities and interests: in this case, the Care in the

Community initiative in which the aim is to get long stay mentally ill and handicapped people out of hospital and prevent the institutionalization of others. This is within a general strategy to decrease the provision of care by the state. It follows that the ability of self help groups for health problems to attract members, to offer support, and to survive was on the agenda of DHSS interests, and the research proposal focused on these issues. However the methodology and attempts to understand self help within broader political and social frameworks was not constrained.

This freedom of approach seems to have been typical of earlier research into self help. However, recently completed and current research has an overtly evaluative component, and thus raises the problems of the representation of different interests by the position taken in the research, and the development of the criteria against which judgements are made.

It is notable that the response of the representatives of Contact a Family to Hatch and Hinton's (1) (1968) analysis and evaluation of their work was broadly favourable. However, they raise this question about the research evidence:

> The mothers' comments recorded by the researchers do indicate the emotional benefits of the support they gained from other mothers. We feel that this is an important result of our facilitating role. Yet it often comes about so informally (for example parents simply ringing each other up) that its significance is difficult to grasp. The measures of outcomes ... suggest that membership of CAF did not have a very strong effect on informal support networks. Hence we wonder whether the measures used were sufficiently sensitive.

The approach of those at the Tavistock Institute of Human Relations who are undertaking research and evaluation of the 18 local support projects managed by the Self Help Alliance (2) (see Stephen Humble, in this publication) can be considered here. They observe that

> Grant-giving bodies increasingly insist on monitoring /evaluation ... (this) does arouse anxieties, some of which are well-grounded; that the evaluator won't fully understand what the project involves; or that there will be over-emphasis or quantitative evaluation of

variables that can be measured, at the expense of more significant factors and processes that can't.

Fortunately the Self Help Alliance was clear that 'the classical model of evaluation, proposing specific outcomes which can be demonstrably linked to particular interventions, and which are amenable to precise measurement' was not appropriate. Rather, the strategy they have adopted is to help local projects to develop self-monitoring and evaluation systems that are useful to projects themselves, as well as contributing data needed for the evaluation of the project as a whole. At this stage in their research they can say that 'most projects are finding that systematic self-evaluation helps them in planning and management, while the role of the research workers seems to be generally experienced as positive and supportive'. It is likely that the interests of support workers are represented in this research.

Similarly, Judith Unell's (3) recognition of the dilemma, constraints and limitations of work in support of self help derives from her evaluation of the work of the Self Help Team in Nottingham. (This is, of course, only part of her contribution, which is broad in scope.) The Team found that 'her work has both enriched our own and made it possible for us to share it with others'.

Evaluative research, like all research, takes a particular position within an agenda of issues not necessarily set by the researcher or those researched. Moreover, the findings will be interpreted and used within wider social and political debates: this aspect will be explored in the next section.

SELF HELP IN BRITAIN: THE DEBATES

The considerations already set out can be illustrated by locating self help for social and health problems within major debates in the field of social policy in Britain. These debates concern the nature of self help, the significance of self help for social policy and practice, and state intervention; each arises because of the particular circumstances of the implementation of the care in the community strategy at a time in which broader government policy is raising questions about the nature of state welfare provision (see Stephen Humble, in this publication). Within each of these debates there are opposed interests and positions which compete to provide the framework of understanding within which research takes place. Each gives rise to different definitions and interpretations of events, sees different 'problems', and implies different policies.

The opposed positions and frameworks for understanding cannot avoid the challenge of empirical studies of self help in the real world. It might seem, on the face of it, that each could demolish the other by appealing to research findings. However, the earlier discussion has pointed out that findings are interpreted and re-interpreted within different explanatory frameworks. The outline of policy debates which follows shows that positions are associated with vested interests in upholding one image of self help as against another, and in pinning particular kinds of expectations to self help activity. Those who wish to make informed judgements need to be aware of the evidence from research - taking account of the framework adopted by the research - and the way it is interpreted when it is deployed in argument. They will then be able to judge if a position can be said to have any basis in empirical investigation. We can now turn to the debates.

The first debate raises questions about the nature of self help. Self help has been welcomed within the care in the community strategy for the practical solutions it can offer and for its place within an ideology which stresses individuals' responsibility for their own lives; a generalized image of self help has developed and has gained wide currency, and there is talk of a self help 'movement'.

The popular image stresses the caring qualities and informality of self help groups. They are seen as a spontaneous response to the need to enhance active mutual caring in a bureaucratized world such that their organization is distinctive and their internal dynamics turn on participation and mutual care. Members give as well as gain social support and greater knowledge of their problem and its management, and their active involvement is presumed to have wider effects on their confidence and social awareness and action. Some commentators speak of a self help movement. This implies not merely that there has been a rapid increase in the number of groups, but that they are in touch with each other, and that there is a coherent philosophy of self help available to them and embraced by them.

However, the popular image is countered by claims by

some researchers that reality is not like this. This position suggests that groups' members include those who do not share the problem as well as those who do; that groups may become rigid in form, with a few givers and many receivers of help; and thus that reciprocity and participation are not necessarily the characteristic patterns of activity. Moreover groups may organize together and create a national level of organization which is bureaucratic in structure; and they may offer services in the mode of a traditional voluntary organization. Nor is it appropriate to speak of a self help movement, for there is no coherent philosophy of self help embraced by most members, and so few of those who might join a group do so.

The opposed positions about the nature of self help are linked with claims about its current and potential contribution to health, social and economic problems. Thus the second debate concerns the significance of self help for social policy and practice. Two polarized positions can be set out in order to make clear the terms of the debate. In the first, self help is seen as an important and significant emergent phenomenon, with its own distinctive way of bringing benefit to many people, and applicable to a wide range of problems. However, the second position suggests that the contribution made by self help is easily over estimated and that it would be inappropriate to invest too many expectations in it. It is not so significant for it reaches comparatively few people, and any significance it has is at the level of political rhetoric rather than practice.

The third debate is concerned with intervention by the state. The question is whether or not self help is something about which the state should have a policy: that is, whether self help is a suitable case for intervention. There are three positions and each rests on an argument about the nature of self help and about the compatibility of an interventionist strategy with the traditional values which underpin social policy in Britain. This reflects the tension between the claims for universalist provision and those for special provision for those with particular problems.

The first position claims that only a non-interventionist stance is legitimate. State funding will enforce a level of formality in self help groups which will at best distort their distinctive nature and contribution and at worse colonize them and make them an arm of the state. Moreover, they are so fragile, so uncertain as to the benefits they bring and so limited as to the people they reach, it is not legitimate to invest public money in them.

The second position supports an interventionist stance. Self help can be supported if sensitive strategies, relevant to its particular needs and avoiding certain pitfalls, are adopted. Further, self help as a form of caring and organizing is important in its own right and should be supported within a tradition in which positive discrimination is possible for those particularly in need.

The third position also supports intervention. In this view, self help is seen not as a form which can survive as a permanent phenomenon, but as a phase in a process of change in which the outcome is service delivery by voluntary organizations of a traditional kind. Intervention and support by the state merely accentuates or speeds up this trend. Indeed it can be seen as a back door way of supporting the development of new voluntary organizations, and may be welcomed as such.

These broad debates form the context within which the particular positions taken by particular interests (the state, medical professions, polemicists of different political persuasions, self help support workers, members of self help groups, and so on) and researchers can be understood.

SELF HELP IN BRITAIN: THE RESEARCH

This review looks at what research can tell us about self help in Britain on a number of issues. Research findings are cited for the different positions they represent - not all researches are set out on each issue. It may be added that this is an under-researched area and, perhaps consequently, high on rhetoric and assertion.

Researchers have looked at different levels of self help organizations and at self help for different ranges of problems. For instance, Levy (1979) (4) attempted to locate and survey mutual support groups in the United Kingdom which were organized around physical, mental and emotional, and social status conditions. Richardson and Goodman (1983) (5) looked at the local groups, members and Head Offices of four organizations with national coverage for broadly social problems. Knight and Hayes (1981) (6) studied self help community initiatives in four inner city areas in London; and (1982) (7) studied nine innovatory economic self help projects. Webb (1982) (8) surveyed self help groups in health, education, welfare, housing, employment and animal care in London; while Vincent (1986) (9) studied self help groups in health care in the Borough of Charnwood and the City of Leicester (in the East Midlands).

There are problems and differences in the way self help is defined. Knight and Hayes contrast Hatch's (1980) (10) approach - 'mutual benefit associations are distinguished by the fact that the main beneficiaries are the members' - with the 'more elaborate definitions' of American writers - e.g. Katz and Bender (1976) (11) self help groups are 'voluntary', small group structures for mutual aid and the accomplishment of a special purpose. They are usually formed by peers who have come together for mutual assistance in satisfying a common need, overcoming a common handicap or life disrupting problem and bringing about desired social, and/or practical change. Richardson and Goodman point out that such definitions exclude many groups ordinarily seen as self help and require extensive knowlege of an organization before it can be given a label. Hence they define self help groups as 'groups of people who feel they have a common problem and have joined together to do something about it', and point out that 'whether they in fact have a common problem, what they do about it and what results are all issues to whch research must be addressed'. An alternative solution adopted in the Charnwood research is to set out the three key components of a 'prescriptive ideal'. That is, all members share the problem; reciprocity is the primary mode of exchange; a commitment to participative democracy informs organizational arrangements. Groups were defined as self help if they had one or more of these features: thus a range of groups was studied and the gap between rhetoric and reality could be observed. Knight and Hayes, similarly, took the seven characteristic features which together form a definition of what constitutes a 'pure' self help group to serve as a model against which actual groups could be compared (see Tina Posner, in this publication). Richardson and Goodman point out that because there are disagreements about definitions 'there is no commonly agreed list of the relevant "population" of such groups'. Thus, while there is agreement that there has been substantial growth in the voluntary sector since the 1960s, and conspicuous growth in self help activity, there is no 'hard' information about this. For instance, the (UK) survey carried out by Levy found 71 groups which met his definition: 12 were local, single-branch groups; 35 were national, multi-branch groups; and 18 were international. On the other hand, Webb's survey in and around London found 2,080 groups, of which 1,515 were concerned with health and welfare. The research in Charnwood found 28 active groups in the field of health care: 15 (54%) had been established since 1980, and 21 (75%) since 1970.

It has been shown that self help groups have a high birth but also a high death rate. Webb's research in London found 87 that had disbanded (of the 2,080 investigated), and the research in Charnwood found seven groups that had folded (against 28 'live' ones). Both these researches refer to the ad hoc and geographically patchy growth of self help groups: the groups in London were mostly in middle class suburban areas; for many, especially the disabled, there is no chance of getting to a group, and for many others the distances and costs of travel are high. The Charnwood research also showed that self help membership represents only a fraction of the potential and is socially and geographically patchy.

Researches show that membership of self help groups in health and social care is predominantly female. There are differences, however, on the question of class: Finch (1984) (12) looked at playgroups run by mothers in economically deprived areas of Lancashire and concluded that playgroups are essentially middle class activities and are doomed in working class areas because they are not what working class women want, need, or are in a position to make work. Richardson and Goodman took housing tenure as a reasonable proxy measure of social class membership and found members roughly similar to the national average distribution 'with the exception of single carers (whose ability to acquire council housing is said to be low)'. The members of groups in Charnwood and Leicester, however, appear to be biased towards the middle class on this measure.

Research does cast some light on the way groups operate in practice: that is, on the issues of participation, democratic organization and commitment to a self help ideology, although again there are differences in interpretation. Robinson and Henry (1977) (13) suggest that those who successfully manage to become members of a self help group accomplish a reorientation to life. D. and Y. Robinson (1979) (14) say that 'The distinctions between helping and being helped, problem-solvers and problem-sufferers, problem-solvers and friends are lost. Self help helping merges into the everyday life of the self help group

members. Self help, in fact, becomes a way of life.'
However, Richardson and Goodman say that members do not
typically join because of some explicit, or even implicit,
desire to support the principle of self help: they join because
they see the group as one of a range of sources of help. They
remain as members for a long while or leave quite soon
because of the nature of their problem. People who have a
sense of identification with, and commitment to, the
particular condition or problem are more likely to stay in a
group - but this may be a far cry from membership bringing
the reconstruction of a new way of life. Nor are the
principles of participation and reciprocity necessarily upheld
in practice. Indeed the research in Charnwood suggests that
groups are best seen along a continuum with 'true' self help
at one pole and traditional service giving, albeit by persons
who share the problem, at the other.

Hatch and Hinton's recently published research set out
(in part) to evaluate Contact a Family's claims that
participation results in changes in the participants'
circumstances and state of mind.

They (like earlier researchers) differentiate between
active and less active members: active members felt their
lives had been changed and expressed commitment to the
self help ideal; less active members valued the more
instrumental activities - the provision of information and
activities for their children. Hatch and Hinton also provide
insight into the differences between members and non-
members: members' children tend to be more handicapped;
members are less likely to belong to ethnic minorities and to
have unskilled jobs; members know about and use services
much more than non-members, and much of their knowledge
was acquired directly or indirectly from their involvement
in CaF. Hatch and Hinton conclude that CaF members are
empowered in three significant ways: through reduced
isolation and becoming part of a supportive network;
through becoming more effective consumers; and through
acting effectively as a group, and that CaF are
indispensable in this process.

CONCLUSION

The evidence from research is necessarily equivocal:
findings turn on concepts and definitions employed within
particular theoretical approaches, and can never be entirely

free of the values and interests of those with the power to commission, frame and fund the research. However, it is possible to take account of these values and interests and to view the findings of research and evaluation in a critical and discerning way. Thus we do not have to say, 'I don't believe in data ...' but we do have to adopt a proper scepticism in our evaluation of research findings. With these constraints in mind, it is possible to make some generalizations about self help in Britain. For instance, that it is a fragile and patchy form of support: that some groups embody the popular image, but many don't; that self help is at the centre of political debates about forms of care and the role of the state in providing them; and that support to self help can subvert its nature and co-opt it in the service of aims defined by others. Research into self help initiatives which combine economic and social goals, as well as that which studies self help groups formed around social and health problems, suggests that the impact of self help is marginal if quantity is measured. Self help initiatives cannot compensate where public provision fails. But the qualitative gains to members are recognized as real and important.

Research is often called upon to adjudicate between political positions, and can be misused and abused in the process. It is necessary for researchers, those researched, and readers and users of research reports to recognize the essentially contested nature of the activity.

NOTES

1.   Stephen Hatch and Teresa Hinton (1986), Self Help in Practice, a study of Contact a Family, community work and family support, Joint Unit for Social Services Research at Sheffield University in collaboration with Community Care, Sheffield.

2.   ARVAC Bulletin, No. 27, Winter, 1986.

3.   Judith Unell, Help for Self Help (1986), Bedford Square Press/NCVO, London.

4.   Leo Levy, Mutual Support Groups in Great Britain: A Survey, Social Sciences and Medicine, Vol. 16, 1982, p. 1265-75.

5.   Ann Richardson and Meg Goodman (1983), Self Help and Social Care: mutual aid organizations in practice, Policy Studies Institute, London.

6.   Barry Knight and Ruth Hayes (1981), Self Help in

the Inner City, London Voluntary Service Council.

7. Barry Knight and Ruth Hayes (1982), The Self Help Economy, London Voluntary Service Council.

8. Penny Webb, Ready, Willing and Able? - the Self Help Group, Journal of the Royal Society of Health, Vol. 103, No. 1, 1983, p. 35-41.

9. Jill Vincent (1986), Constraints on the Stability and Longevity of Self Help Groups in the Field of Health Care, Report to the DHSS.

10. Stephen Hatch (1980), Outside the State, Croom Helm, London.

11. Alfred H. Katz and Eugene I. Bender (1976), The Strength in Us: Self Help Groups in the Modern World, New Viewpoints, New York.

12. Janet Finch, The Deceit of Self Help: Pre-School Playgroups and Working Class Mothers, Journal of Social Policy, 13, 1, 1984, p. 1-20.

13. David Robinson and Stuart Henry (1977), Self Help and Health: Mutual Aid for Modern Problems, Martin Robertson, London.

14. David Robinson and Yvonne Robinson (1979), From Self Help to Health, Concord Books, London.

Chapter Six

WHY WE NEED DATA: OBSERVATIONS ON EVALUATION RESEARCH IN HEALTH-RELATED SELF HELP

Dieter Grunow

INTRODUCTION

Evaluation seems to be a widely accepted scientific tool for the description of activities (interventions) and their effects on the addressed population. This includes the health sector as many others. It seems to be reasonable to extend evaluative questions also into the self help activities of the population. But this does not mean that there are no 'specifics' to be considered in this context. It is the attempt of this paper to explore some of these 'specifics' of evaluative research in the self help field.

As 'evaluation' often seems to be accompanied by scientific-professional mystification and by anxieties among the evaluated parties, it is necessary to give some general orientation of what 'evaluation' means. In very basic terms evaluation is a review of the results (effects) of activities which are initiated to obtain these (or at least 'some') results.

Evaluation is a very pervasive element in the everyday activities of human beings. It can even be described as one of the basic features which differentiates between mankind and all other living creatures. We are able to look for the consequences of our actions, and we try to change them in order to obtain other results. Thus, evaluation is not the invention of some researchers but an everyday practice of us all. The difference made by scientific evaluators concerns
-   the transparency of the evaluation procedure
-   the quality of the necessary observation (i.e. reliability)

- the soundness of the interpretation of evaluative observations/findings

It is a well-known fact from existing experiences that the impact of evaluation might be greater in making the actors aware of their hidden goals and practical theories (about proper ways of goal achievement) than in reviewing specific impact measures (see: Freeman/Solomon 1982). This is not simply the result of the ignorance and incompetence of the actors but very often is caused by the complexity of the action context and the lack of 'distance' of the actors from the activities which are to be evaluated. To include 'third parties' (e.g. researchers) into evaluation processes, therefore, can be an important step to sort out possible or probable action consequences and to clarify inter-dependencies between action elements.

Evaluation in the health field is of great relevance because 'health' in general is an important element of good living conditions. It is also an area in which wrong actions can easily lead to fatal consequences. The lay health system is extensively engaged in practical evaluation procedures, because:

it is confronted with so many propositions/ads about 'adequate health-related behaviour'

it is the place where the consequences are perceived /suffered

Although the medical system provides many tests of health/illness status, it relies heavily on the observations of the lay person/patient. This is especially true in a situation where professional services cover only a small portion of the health problems of the individual and where each profession has its own (additional) selectivity. The individual, then, is the most important reference point (a) for summing up the actions taken (eventually by many different persons /specialists) and (b) for registration of the effects on his/her health status.

Within the medical system evaluation procedures seem to be well established. But a critical review reveals that there are also many deficiencies. As it is extremely difficult to either sort out or to exclude complex interdependencies, evaluation issues are often too narrow in their scope - following a model of laboratory testing (i.e. tests of drugs). Another aspect of these deficiencies is the evaluation of the 'success' of general practitioners. There have been only a few attempts to evaluate their therapeutic activities at all (Senftleben 1980; Sechrest 1985). There are also many indications that major (historical) changes in the health status of the population were not the result of better medical treatment - as claimed hastily by the professionals - but the effect of basic changes in living conditions (see McKeown 1979).

These observations lead us to the conclusion that, while accepting the notion of evaluation in the self help context, there is no reason to look to the medical system for guidelines of good practice and adequate procedures (including the definition of quality standards). Referring to the title, it can be said that WE NEED DATA to make self help activities better perceived in quantity and quality and to clarify their standards of good practice. Under such conditions evaluative research can be seen as an offer of support to self help initiatives.

But, with this perspective of evaluative research, scientific projects are the objects of different and antagonistic forces in our societies in the same way as self help initiatives are. It is necessary for both types of activities (self help and research) to describe and take into account the political and institutional context of their activities. This will be done in the next paragraph. It is related to features of the German health system and of the German research funding system. More specific considerations about possibilities and restrictions on evaluation research in health-related self help will follow in the second section.

SELF HELP AND RELATED RESEARCH IN THE GERMAN HEALTH CARE SYSTEM

The necessity to refer to the institutional background of self help initiatives seems to be contradicted by the fact that, in countries with different context-configurations, similar (or even the same) phenomena are observed. Although this might lead to a discourse about the international diffusion of ideas, concepts and practical initiatives - beyond all structural differences - some additional arguments are important. In our complex societies it is difficult to make an issue a topic of general and continuous public concern. A typical precondition is the diffusiveness of the topic and its ability to serve many (symbolic and/or practical) functions. It explains why similar initiatives and ideologies can develop under different circumstances. A typical example is the idea of 'self help in health' and the 'self help movement' in many countries. It is evidently related to some basic needs of the population and some deficiencies of health-related living conditions and services. But at the same time it carries many meanings and fulfils many ends. These multi-dimensional and multifunctional aspects of the self help movement make it possible that different organizations and groups claim the name 'self help group'. The medical professions claim their competence in organizing self help initiatives, as does the public health administration. Alternative medical practice is 'sold' under the heading of 'help for self help'. Thus, it is hardly surprising to observe similar - or at least similarly named - initiatives emerging in different countries (with a different institutional background.)

But, in spite of this, in our opinion it is still worthwhile to look at these background characteristics with regard to more specific questions of the development of self help in the respective countries: there might still be important differences to be found. For the German case, I would like to stress the following points (for details see the paper of Matzat in this volume).

During the development of the German welfare system there were always ambivalent opinions about state interventions into these affairs; there were many initiatives coming from churches and voluntary organizations as well as from the unions and the workers' movement. Although these institutions are nowadays widely dependent on public funds, they claim to be a counterpart of the state and part of the self help potential. Historically speaking the self help movement has predecessors (in the context of workers' solidarity, self-organization and subsidary), but in the recent situation these institutions are often rather 'strange bedfellows' of self help initiatives. The self help movement, thus, has to be seen in a 'triangle' with the state and voluntary organizations - whereby the latter try to reinforce their (power) position vis-a-vis the state by 'incorporating' the self help initiatives.

The configuration is completed by a fourth powerful component: the medical profession (and other professions). The state has not only given extensive autonomy to the private medical service system but has also installed a non-market system of financing services, in which the medical profession has major influence. Thus, the monopoly of the medical profession is not only based on (claimed or real) expertise (monopoly for treatment of patients) but also on exclusive access to financial resources (of the health insurances). Only lately have efforts been made to control the latter element of the power position. It is easy to anticipate the importance of this feature for the development and the antagonisms self help initiatives face: the medical profession not only defines which service is adequate for the patient but also how the money of the health insurances is spent (for him/her). Not at all surprising, therefore, is the claim of the medical profession that it is its task to define allowable forms of self help and the quality standards to be applied to them.

The state - although still holding the overall responsibility for the health status of the population - has confined itself to the formulation of the legal framework and to the provision of the financial means for the welfare system. The increasing criticism against economization and bureaucratization of the welfare system has led to the adoption of service strategies - which reinforce the growth of professional competence as well as its dominance, and do not even reduce bureaucratization. Thus, self help initiatives are 'observed' by state institutions with a mixture of rule-related scepticism and of hopes for cheap solutions to otherwise costly health problems.

To summarize: in spite of similarities in the surface phenomena of self help initiatives, there are unique background phenomena in the German situation which explain recent developments and which throw a peculiar light on future possibilities and restrictions of the self help movement in the health field. At the same time it indicates different interests concerning research topics:

for the medical system it is still the question of patient compliance, the identification of malpractice in the lay-system or the establishing of the same quality criteria (e.g. effects measured by the technical instruments used; morbidity rates; mortality rates etc.)

for the voluntary associations it is the interest in showing that they are the 'better' self help groups, because they 'integrate' dissenting groups and at the same time guarantee rule following settlement of (public) accounts

for the public administration it is the interest in knowing how one could save money by referring to the potential of self help initiatives

It is important to clarify the aims of evaluative research and the 'interested parties' of it in order to judge the usefulness of the self help initiatives themselves. In many instances there will be domain and dominance conflicts between the funders and initiators of research and lay initiatives.

HEALTH RELATED RESEARCH AND THE GERMAN SCIENCE SYSTEM

To do evaluative research in health related self help issues does not only interfere in domains and vested interests of actors from health-related professions and service institutions. It might also affect the scientific background and knowledge about health-related issues. It might use up research sources, and it might come to question traditional theories and findings.

To describe the 'gatekeepers' of these resources and the 'trend- or standard-setters' for scientific inquiries is an important prerequisite for the understanding of possibilities and limits of evaluative research in this field.

In Germany, there is an extended overlapping area between the earlier mentioned actors of the medical system and the science system (including their funding). In all relevant decision-contexts, the medical profession plays a dominant role: in university based research, in the review of applications for research funds and in the setting up of state-initiated experimental models (and accompanying research). Although health-related issues could be partially a domain of social scientists, there is no (not yet any) substantive health-related research capacity in Germany which is not dependent on the 'good will' of the medical profession.

The subject areas of social medicine, epidemiology or medical sociology are mainly part of the medical faculties in German universities. An independent sociological research into health or even into medicine is almost impossible. There have been a few attempts by the Social Democratic party in the seventies to fund such research. It was ended after only a few years - and not only because of the change of the government in 1982. Sociological questions are since then (again) closely tied to illness-related research which is defined by the medical profession (see Forschung und Entwicklung im Dienst der Gesundheit 1983).

In the fundgiving institutions (DFG, Stiftung

Volkswagenwerk, Boschstiftung - to name only a few important ones) the medical profession defines not only the topics but also the standards for scientific undertakings. It can be interpreted as an important strategy for the protection of domains in professional service production. The topic of self help (devalued as 'bungling of laypeople') and the idea of evaluation are not supported if they don't follow the predefinitions of medical professionals.

Some interest in evaluative research exists on the side of the government, because the cost increase in the medical system is a permanent issue. Here, new models of health services are tested (by evaluative research) and/or some hopes about less expensive solutions to health problems via self help initiatives are put forward. The question of a better health status for the population or the general importance of the lay system are only of marginal interest. Only the idea of self help groups has received some attention. But the funds which are given to this field of concern are not even a measurable proportion of 1% of the research money given to clinical medical investigations. The same is true for the whole field of welfare services: not even a tenth part of 1% of the money spent in this system is given to (evaluative) research - although there is a long list of complaints about ineffectiveness, inefficiency and little consumer-orientation (a long list of authors gives evidence: Achinger, v. Ferber, Liefmann-Keil, Kaufmann, Badura and others).

In conclusion, it can be said that there are important actors in the field of defining and financing scientific investigations who are not interested in research about self help issues in health or in <u>health</u> (in contrast to <u>illness</u>) altogether. Thus, evaluative research in this sphere has to face many forms of restrictions and practical obstacles. This might even develop the image of a trap; we need data to overcome some of the one-sided perspectives and the definition-power of the medical system; but it is hard to get this information because it is the same system (persons and institutions) which controls large parts of fund distribution and the definition of research questions.

EVALUATING SELF HELP IN HEALTH

Goals, vested interests and quality standards

In spite of the very diffuse definition of self help in German public debate, the following considerations will be restricted to a more specific view. The fundamental difference which self help initiatives are introducing into the health system is confined to informal everyday activities in primary social networks and autonomous self help groups. They consist of activities which cannot be substituted by other means and institutions and/or they rely on contrasting sets of personal perplexity and experience. The other - often more organized and professionalized - forms of 'self help' initiatives are or soon become similar to any service organization (with features like bureaucracy and professional orientation) or to any lobby organization. (The evaluation of these more organized forms of self help is described by Vincent in this volume.) The emphasis on informal forms of self help does not imply a value judgement about other forms. Often the more organized form is developed out of the informal initiatives - as argued by Posner in this volume.

For evaluation research the forms of self help under consideration make important differences in terms of goals, methods used and expected outcomes. This is the main reason why the following arguments are confined to the narrow conception of informal self help as described above.

As has been described in the preceding chapters, these less visible and rather contingent forms of self help are not protected from political bureaucratic and professional influences or even pressures. In the perspective of politicians self help initiatives should provide cheap alternatives to cure and care provision in the health system (especially nursing care for sick and/or old people at home). Administrators try to keep control over activities by introducing rules of legally sound practice and proper ways of fund utilization; they contribute to setting up all kinds of small organizations for this purpose - including the clearing houses, which in the second generation of staff will become administratively controlled forms of self help 'provision' and co-ordination. The medical profession tries to define 'allowable' and 'adequate' self help or even tries (now) to include self help groups in its own catalogue of compliant behaviour. Thus informal forms of self help are often asked to conform with the goals and quality criteria of actors and institutions, against (in opposition to) which self help initiatives have been developed. A paradoxical situation with a probably counterproductive outcome.

It is an important task of evaluative research to identify the different aims of relevant actors and to help to identify the goals of those people and groups which are engaged in informal self help activities. It is one important lesson from previous evaluation research that it is not sufficient to restrict its task to effect - or success-measurement (Stufflebeam 1978; Freeman/Solomon 1982). It is necessary to include process descriptions and evaluations as well - the so-called formative evaluation (Rossi/Freeman 1985). Especially during the process of goal-development - definition evaluators can acquire an important catalytic function - and quite independent of the degree of formality/informality with which the goal setting is practically realized.

Our own research in families (Grunow et al 1983, 1984) has shown that there are often very unclear and, among family members, very controversial, ideas about what could/should be done with regard to informal everyday self help. In many instances the interview situation was the first occasion at which family members exchanged their respective views on this matter! With regard to self help groups this might be somewhat different because they are not a part of everyday activities. To initiate or participate in such a group demands more explicit aims and expected outcomes. But - as some observations of the Hamburg project show - these are all but clear or consensual, and they might change drastically over time. There are many instances where some 'informal' leaders start to dominate the self help group by imposing their personal views on the rest of the group (Halves et al 1987).

In sum, evaluative research in the phase of goal setting and goal revision in informal self help contributes in at least three ways:

showing the origins of externally imposed goals and outcome expectations and their (institutional and/or professional) protagonists;

helping to clarify the implicit aims of those engaged in informal self help as well as their attempts to set their own standards of good practice;

identifying important reference points for further steps of evaluative research.

It is not necessary to exclude all 'other directed' claims

on the capacity and quality of informal self help, but it is necessary to confront these claims with the interests and possibilities of the people concerned. There are probably very specific features of self help to be dealt with in the first place:

the offering of socio-psychic support;

the availability of experiences from persons/groups with similar health-related difficulties;

the ability to integrate health related self help into everyday routines;

the ability to re-organize complex action environments (like the general way of living);

the ability to incorporate the 'necessities' of health related problems into life plans;

the fact that the group activities <u>as such</u> might be a sufficient 'outcome' for self help initiatives;

the fact that equal status and reciprocity in communication among group members might be a more important issue than to deal with the specifics of a chronic illness;

and many other elements.

RESEARCH PROCEDURES AND METHODS

It is quite clear that the specifics of self help activities and their underlying goals must also be acknowledged in the design of evaluative research. As described above, evaluation is not an activity invented by scientists or researchers. And, in addition, evaluation is not an activity which is connected with a specific institutional and professional outfit (researchers, research funds, research organizations etc.). Whereas the general idea of evaluation might be the same, the concrete design of evaluation research <u>differs</u> according to the subject matter. The same methods <u>cannot</u> be successfully applied to clinical drug testing, performance analysis of bureaucratic welfare institutions and informal self help. This is the consequence of different aims and (predominantly) of the different circumstances of lay activities.

In general one could say that evaluation in the informal self help setting is devoted

to qualitative goals and outcomes (rather than to quantitative measures)

to subjective indicators (i.e. judgements of the

participating persons) rather than to objective indicators - which often are not all objective either, as the attempts to increase the precision of diagnoses show)
- to procedural questions rather than to concrete effects measurement (see Posner in this volume)
- to non-reactive (in part participatory) methods rather than to reactive standardized methods.

The reasons for this accentuation have been mentioned already: (a) aims and quality standards for informal activities are not always consciously considered and defined: they are 'buried' in everyday routines and often must be made conscious again; (b) self help is often a latent phenomenon, not in effect for a while, but suddenly necessary and active again; (c) self help (especially self help groups) is a very dynamic/fluctuating phenomenon sometimes with only a short life, with changing aims and fluctuating membership; (d) self help is - at least in part - a reaction to the structure and performance of the medical system; it also changes with changes in the system.

In sum, all this demands a very specific evaluative research design. It is a small scale, participatory and qualitative kind of evaluation. It has more similarities with practice-oriented monitoring than with highly professionalized research projects. Some of the necessary methodological tools still have to be developed - hence one might concentrate on the 'grounded theory' approach (see Glaser 1978). This approach also offers ways of theory building - which (to me) seems the most promising way in researching informal self help. Its acceptance as an adequate approach will have to be defended against the contention that all relevant measures of self help capacity have to be standardized and quantitative.

LIMITATIONS AND DIFFICULTIES

Since the myths of the infallibility of medical professionals have diminished it has become more evident to them, as well as to their customers, that evaluation not only registers successes but also identifies failures. Thus, the interest and demand for (more) evaluation in the health field is at least ambivalent. Within the professional system this seems to be because the potential of evaluative research is known; in the lay sector there is such ambivalence because not enough is known about its potential.

Limitations and difficulties do not only stem from the defence of professional domains or from the competition for programme research funds. There are also restrictions inherent in the subject matter and in the acting persons or groups. Questions of health and illness, although somehow everybody's concern, are also very personal and intimate affairs. People often do not want to carry these topics into the public domain and/or do not want to answer questions about them. Often they are only willing to mention such issues under strict anonymity - as the examples of AA groups and telephone advisers demonstrate.

To apply non-reactive or even participatory methods is difficult and sometimes inhibited as well. Participation in a self help group is a valuable method to obtain relevant data, but groups often do not want 'outsiders' in their group, because this always has an impact on group activities. On the other hand, the observer might 'go native', change the nature of documentation, stop it altogether or be unwilling to make his data available to other researchers.

The research project, therefore, might produce materials which are not easily assessed with reference to authenticity, relevance and production procedure. At least, the findings often will have to be judged as special and (more or less) unique pieces of evidence. They are not easily generalized. This is a general problem of intensive qualitative research methods: the more detailed and relevant the data that are won, the more difficult it is to go beyond a case description and to arrive at some more generalized conclusions. This is also true in other research contexts (where qualitative methods are applied), but often there are additional quantitative data available. Besides some informal aspects a formal structure might also be a reference point in evaluative research. In the context of informal self help (and especially in self help groups) these additions or partial substitutes are very rare. But, nevertheless, as the reference to 'grounded theory' has indicated, there are ways to build up theoretical concepts and knowledge on the basis of such research findings.

With regard to the above described functions of evaluative research in the self help context it is quite possible that some of the results are only important for the participants. It only gives them some clues on recent activities and their effects. Thus, it must be acknowledged that some of the important results of such a project cannot be (easily) 'sold' to the larger scientific community or to the

85

fundgiving institutions. Some compromises with regard to the selected evaluation design might be inevitable.

It is quite possible that the demands of fundgiving institutions cannot be combined with the interest of the people engaged in self help activities. It is necessary to have some small scale tools available for them which they can use to improve their self-control and self-evaluation. The autonomy of these persons or groups includes their right to refuse an evaluation from the very beginning or to stop it during its application. Again, it is necessary to make fundgivers and scientists aware of this condition of evaluative research. To avoid such unexpected ruptures it is especially important in this 'contingent research situation' to sort out clearly the different interests implied in the evaluation before it begins: i.e. the public at large, politicians, fundgiving institutions, actors with vested interests in the health field, the scientific community, the research team, self help actors and their social environment. Many evaluation projects will not be started at all; those which start will have better chances to be carried through, notwithstanding the changes which will be made during the course of evaluation. This is a final point of foreseeable conditions of the evaluation of self help. Much more than in other research fields one has to adjust to many changes during the course of evaluation because of changes in the activities, the participants and the context of self help. It is also an expectation which has to be communicated to other institutions interested in the evaluation.

In sum, evaluative research in the informal self help setting has still to develop parts of its methodological tools. It is far away from a completely specified and obligatory set of research steps, which ultimately lead to a reliable, valid and generalizable result.

CONCLUSIONS: WHY DO WE NEED DATA?

Although self help activities in health often include very specific biographical and personal prerequisites and circumstances, it nevertheless makes sense to pass information and to share experiences between different groups of the population. For this reason it is necessary to document, compare and evaluate relevant information - in other words: to produce data. This does not necessarily mean to set up a big evaluation 'machinery'. In many cases it can be done with little resources. But it implies a more conscious dealing with information than 'practitioners' of all kinds do. It is a well known fact that the 'Vordringlichkeit des Befristeten' (priority for those who are disadvantaged) as well as the tendency to avoid 'uber den eigenen Tellerrand zu blicken' (looking beyond one's own domain) preoccupies the environment. This is one reason why the role of conscious and controlled data collection and interpretation is often separated from the participants and/or the addressees of health related activities.

Evaluative data in the sense described above are first of all needed by lay people in the health system. There is a need to compare and validate experiences of other persons (with the same or similar problems). Somewhat methodical and systematic data gathering is necessary to make people aware of their own starting-point. (In our research we have often received favourable comments on instruments - like health diaries which help people to describe and review their everyday behaviour. In addition - rather unexpectedly - many partners of in-depth interviews asked for a copy of the transcription because they felt they had never described and reflected on their situation in such a concentrated and detailed form before).

In the context of new initiatives (like self help groups) data about other initiatives, their goals and their effects are important points of orientation and help to clarify one's own aims and the ambitions of external actors and forces. It is also a prerequisite for the review of possible outcomes for the participants and for a realistic description of the potential of such groups - an important point of orientation for irresolute or hesitating (potential!) members of self help groups.

The second set of demands for evaluation data comes from interested and influential outsiders. In spite of all autonomy in everyday self help and informal groups, there are many influences which make it ever more difficult to claim competence and autonomy for the lay system. Whenever a specific (moral, legal, financial) support is demanded from outsiders, the necessity to argue on the basis of data is even more important. As many relevant decisions are based on systematically documented activities and their effects on health status or its improvement, the presentation of some solid data plays an important part in bargaining processes. If one does not want to leave the field to the medical profession, the state or to voluntary welfare institutions, and if one does not want to leave the definition of standards for good practice to the medical professionals, a data-based participation in these public and scientific debates is necessary. The available material for Germany is still very meagre. The recent chances to broaden the systematic and empirical foundation of lay activities and competences in the health sector are very small.

Part Four

LOCAL SUPPORT FOR SELF HELP

INTRODUCTORY NOTE

Judith Unell

The papers in this section are written by people with considerable practical experience of supporting local self help groups. Together they address this subject from a number of perspectives.

They describe the environment within which local support centres or clearing houses have developed in each country (Matzat and Unell). In both England and West Germany, widespread recognition of self help groups and their need for support has grown out of the work of imaginative local projects which have responded to self help in their areas. The creation of regional and national networks of support workers has been the next phase in the development of self help support, strengthening and publicizing local work. These networks have also brought the issues surrounding self help to the attention of government. The need to influence and monitor government action, particularly in the distribution of funds, has been a common concern in both countries. Strategies have been devised to try to ensure that government initiatives work to the advantage of self help groups but many tensions remain.

Alongside this general discussion of the history and future direction of self help support, there are accounts of two specific local support centres - KISS in Hamburg and The Self Help Team in Nottingham (Estorff, Wilson, Unell). Their history, their current work and their approach to the task of supporting local groups are considered, and some wider lessons are drawn about the practical dilemmas for support centres of adopting the role of facilitators rather than leaders in their contacts with self help groups.

In focusing upon projects with a specific brief to

support self help, it is important not to ignore the vital contribution which can be made by a range of other organizations in helping groups to begin and survive. Indeed, most 'specific' support centres would see the promotion of the concept of self help support among other agencies as a central aspect of their work. Helmut Brietkopf discusses the potential contribution to self help of medical practitioners, hospitals and clinics, adult education centres, health insurance companies and others in a position to enhance and extend the work of self-help support centres. Changes in structures and training programmes would be needed before this contribution could be recognized but, most of all, there needs to be a more general recognition of the value of self help and of its need for support and encouragement.

Chapter Seven

ON SUPPORT FOR SELF HELP GROUPS AT THE LOCAL LEVEL

Jürgen Matzat and Astrid Estorff

In 1977 the German Federal Government, through the Federal Ministry of Youth, Family and Health, began a research project at the University Hospital for Psychosomatic Illness and Psychotherapy at Giessen. The purpose of this project was to obtain more precise knowledge of the way self help groups work, and to test possible ways of encouraging the formation of such groups and supporting them. The project developed into an important early nucleus about which the 'new' self help movement crystallized. This term refers to those collective attempts at self help which came into being outside established welfare organizations, traditional associations for the disabled and pattern of groups such as Alcoholics Anonymous and Gamblers Anonymous.

The research team had direct contact with the groups and persons concerned, and its activities led to the setting up of the first support service for self help groups on a local level. The experiences of the Giessen team were published in the project report and in numerous articles, and were the subject of many talks, and they provided a pattern for many professionals who, in the years that followed, took on the task of providing contact centres for self help groups in their own towns. These initiatives varied in form, depending on particular local conditions, their professional qualifications and the concerns of the institutions they worked for. The Giessen project increasingly became known throughout West Germany, not only amongst professionals, but to a wider public. As a result people throughout the country took to writing to Giessen to seek information about how self help groups worked or to ask for the addresses of groups which they themselves could join.

Of course the team was completely swamped by these enquiries. They were able to do little except produce standard information material for interested persons, since only at the local level is it possible to provide concrete support for the work of self help groups, particularly for the formation of new groups - and at that time the number of existing groups was far fewer than today. A popular concept for this in Germany is 'Gemeindenähe' - being close to the community - which is seen as an indispensable requirement for almost any medical or other social work with mentally ill, chronically sick, elderly or disturbed clients.

There was a further problem. The few self help groups that already existed outside the region of Giessen were unknown to the researchers there. One essential feature of the new 'self help group movement' is that people join together with a minimum of formal organization. Often they do not have any formal structure, they are not part of any large umbrella organization, and there is no register of their contacts. They form a garland of varied and colourful flowers, but on the whole they blush unseen. Enquiries by the team at Giessen amongst their colleagues in social work with the ill and disturbed, and in medicine in other towns showed that most were astonishingly ill-informed about existing or newly formed self help activities in their regions.

All this made it impossible for the Giessen project to give direct, permanent and meaningful support to people involved with self help groups - neither, in particular, to those who were or might become members of groups, and their relatives, nor to experts working with them. Much more useful was to bring about increased interest in this new field of work on the part of professionals and appropriate institutions - and also on the part of already experienced members of self help groups - and to obtain their co-operation. The more such 'contact centres' or 'Regional Working Associations' (Regional Arbeitsgemein-schaften), as we first called them, came into being, the more people would have the chance, on neutral ground, of meeting professionally competent partners with whom they could first have a personal discussion to clarify their needs, plans, hopes and fears concerning self help groups, and who would then accompany and support them in the concrete activities of starting a group and sustaining its work.

Those who took part in the Giessen project were also strongly motivated by another aspect. At that time, they were the first and only people involved in working out a theoretical understanding and practical methods for the support of self help groups at a local level. This gave them a keen interest in getting to know colleagues elsewhere who were also beginning to gather experiences and undertake assessment, with a view to exchanging ideas with them and making further development possible.

In the course of time these efforts brought into being a network of colleagues interested and to an increasing degree experienced in the subject, who besides their routine work concerned themselves with stimulating and supporting self help groups in their own communities: the German Working Association for the Support of Self Help Groups (Deutsche Arbeitsgemeinschaft Selbsthilfegruppen). At that time many of its members worked in university institutes and research projects. At the beginning the academic and professional element was very strongly represented. But there was also participation from practitioners from counselling centres and medical institutions, and also by particularly committed members of self help groups. What was common to them all was their great interest and a distinctive motivation, perhaps even a kind of 'philosophy'. In any case it was something more than, or different from, the ordinary job at which they earned their living.

Since then the Deutsche Arbeitsgemeinschaft Selbsthilfegruppen has registered as a charitable association and has become an established influence in the discussion of self help in West Germany. Apart from providing a national information service about self help groups, producing appropriate pamphlets and leaflets, and answering a wide range of questions from potential or actual group members and professionals, an increasingly important task over the years has been helping to set up local contact and information centres (clearing houses) and to support them in their work. To this end the experiences which have been culled with such effort over the years were drawn together and brought into a system. The main functions of such a local clearing house are:

Counselling to individuals with an interest in self help, and where necessary putting them in touch with appropriate self help groups.

Support in setting up new self help groups, where there are not any in the locality for a particular kind of problem, or where the existing groups are currently unable to accept new members.

Skilled advice to existing groups about their work, especially in matters such as group dynamics and the group process.

Establishing contact between self help groups and professional experts so that they can co-operate.

Keeping the public informed about self help groups and the creation of a social climate that encourages their work.

Providing or organizing practical help such as meeting rooms, office facilities, etc.

It is often best to set up a specific organization to carry out these functions, but they can also be attached to existing bodies. All that matters is that these functions are carried out in a defined region, and that in time the staff responsible become qualified by the acquisition of the necessary skills. In West Germany this approach has largely been developed within the framework of the Deutsche Arbeitsgemeinschaft Selbsthilfegruppen, and the Arbeitsgemeinschaft has organized the exchange of experience and the training of workers, so that its accumulated knowledge can be passed on.

These tasks - national information, encouraging development, creating a social climate and training and development, have also been carried out since 1984 by a project under the auspices of the Deutsche Arbeitsgemeinschaft Selbsthilfegruppen. This project is in Berlin, and employs three staff with financial support from the Berlin Provincial Government. It is known as the Nationale Kontakt- und Informationsstelle zur Anregung und Unterstutzung von Selbsthilfegruppen (NAKOS - the National Contact and Information Centre - 'Clearing House' - for the Development and Support of Self Help Groups).

The idea of support for self help groups by local contact and information centres has been taken up by many organizations in West Germany in the last few years. Not only 'Krankenkassen' (the national and local organizations that administer health insurance), but also large welfare organizations, local councils and small local voluntary associations, have become active and provide this kind of support. The Deutsche Arbeitsgemeinschaft Selbsthilfegruppen and NAKOS are aware of and work with more than 100 local contact centres in the German Federal Republic and West Berlin.

This growth is naturally to be welcomed. On the other hand, it is almost impossible to assess the kind of service that lies behind these addresses. For some time not all who support self help groups have joined the network that has grown up, to profit from the traditions created within it. Instead their loyalties lie much more than in the past with their employers, associations and sponsors. Moreover, the motivation of many newer workers in the field (or their institutions) is not the same as before. It is no longer so strongly characterized by a primary concern with self help groups and their development, and by a fascination with what lay persons, non-professionals, can achieve collectively under certain circumstances, and for the most part without the direct involvement of professionals. More recently, there has been a stronger emphasis on the part played by professionals, on advice to others with the same problem, and on the financial arrangements to sustain this kind of service provision. There is already discussion - especially in the sphere of the voluntary social service associations and publicly funded social work - about whether self help groups, or co-operation with them, is a 'new method of social work'. And if this is so, the obvious next step is for professionals to re-establish their rights and standing in this field. And then - the more so since Germany is a country with a pluralist structure for providing care - the institutions will compete to get their hands as fast as possible, before the others, on staff and funds for this new field of work. For many, the field of self help is seen as the last growth area in a social market threatened by a policy of cuts.

Besides this, the concepts of self help and self help groups have an extraordinarily positive aura in present-day West Germany. This makes them very useful for building up your image. Institutions which support self help groups are seen as progressive, tolerant, and close to the grass roots. Who would miss the chance of a reputation of that kind?

But the greatest problem created by this flavour of the month is the technical qualification and experience of local workers. In many cases they are recruited through job creation programmes which save the sponsor of the activity a great deal of money. But the result is that for the most part very young workers are appointed, often at the beginning of their career, without any experience in social work with the ill, elderly or disturbed, let alone in the field of self help in the narrower sense. And their job comes to an end after one or at the most two years, just when they have somehow managed to teach themselves how to do it. This of course makes personal continuity, a vital necessity for work with self help groups, virtually impossible.

The same problems occur when such posts are staffed by persons doing the work as an alternative to military service. In West Germany, where military service is universal, they too are regarded as a cheap supplement to scarce staff in social work and health care.

The point must be made, that even though there is a very considerable number of support services in West Germany, very few of them have yet succeeded in ensuring sufficient staff and running costs on a permanent basis. One of the most experienced and firmly established is that in Hamburg.

Chapter Eight

THE CONTACT AND INFORMATION CENTRE FOR SELF HELP GROUPS IN HAMBURG: HOW IT WAS SET UP

Astrid Estorff

The Kontakt- und Informationsstelle für Selbsthilfegruppen (KISS) has existed since January 1981. It was set up as an experimental model project within the research project on self help groups in the field of health conducted by the Medical Sociology Department. It was located in the University Hospital at Hamburg-Eppendorf, with one member of staff and one student assistant. The purpose of setting up this model unit was to carry out action research into the support and encouragement of self help groups and to encourage the setting-up of new groups by means of a contact centre.

Just before the conclusion of the research project, at the end of 1983, we applied to the Hamburg Health Authority for finance to carry on the Contact and Information Centre as an independent entity. The application was approved. The sponsor of the Centre was the association called Sozialwissenschaften und Gesundheit - 'Social sciences and health'. The one and a half full-time equivalent posts were shared between three workers whose professional qualifications were in sociology, social education and education. Since then staffing has increased to two full-time equivalent posts and a further worker is there as an alternative to military service.

When we began to plan a service to promote and support self help groups, our starting point was the idea that it was important for its growth to be steady and cautious. We constantly reconsidered whether, and to what extent, it was useful and necessary to give support to groups. We wanted to react to needs and requirements, and not to create them through the Centre itself. We had already developed this point of view during the previous years. Our basic opinion is that in the field of self help professional workers should not undertake, without reservation, the role of a 'promoter'. Instead, they should react with caution to the needs, as they become apparent, of those involved in self help, the founders of groups and the groups themselves.

Since the middle of 1984 the Contact Centre has worked in premises of its own in the 'Werkhof' Centre for Alternative Activities. This change of location brought several essential ideas to reality. Access to the new organization had to be easy, and its premises suitable for the disabled. Besides this, facilities had to exist for people to have contact and to be together with other human beings outside individual groups. The Werkhof, with its many groups and initiatives, as well as a bar and an ice cream parlour, was almost ideal in all these respects. One of the main themes of the project and the Contact Centre is at once made visible and concrete, its slogan: 'Gemeinsam sind wir stärker - We are stronger together.' In addition, the Contact Centre intends to use its location to act as an intermediary in another way. It endeavours to bring about contact and communication between the project groups which stand for concepts of wholeness in life and health (e.g. health food shops, Network, Robin Hood, food co-operatives and so on) and their users.

Besides offices for the Contact Centre staff there are three rooms in which self help groups can meet. This facility has been used by groups on more than 800 occasions in the last twelve months.

AIMS AND OBJECTIVES OF THE CONTACT CENTRE

The aims which we have set out for our work and the objectives that result from this have arisen from the experience of the first two years. One essential aim of the Contact Centre is to create a public climate which encourages and motivates people to take more and more responsibility for their own health, and no longer to leave concern and decisions about health and sickness solely to the professionals. This is often the first step which leads people into a self help group. To achieve this, we try to inform interested lay people and professionals about the work of self help groups and how they go about it, and to encourage them to be active themselves or to stimulate self help groups in their own professional fields.

Besides this very general aim, the Contact and Information Centre has set itself the objective of acting as a kind of general post office for all self help activities related to health in the Hamburg area. We understand health in the sense of the definition of the World Health Organization, 'Health is a state of physical, mental and social well-being, and not only the absence of disease and disability.' Thus we set out to provide a service not only to those involved in self help, and to self help groups, but also to collect and distribute information to health care professionals, to researchers and to those responsible for health at the political level.

Our activity can be divided into the following main areas of emphasis:

1. Giving advice to those involved in self help and work with self help groups.
2. Giving general information about self help and the associated publicity work.
3. Giving information about, and work with, interested health care professionals.

GIVING ADVICE TO THOSE INVOLVED WITH SELF HELP AND WORK WITH SELF HELP GROUPS

Maintaining the directory of self help groups

A central part of our work is maintaining the directory of groups. This contains details of the self help groups in the Hamburg area known to us, together with the most important agencies providing counselling and psychiatric social work. Once a year a phone call is made to every group in the directory, to make sure that the information we are passing on is up-to-date. In the field of self help this is particularly important, since its informal nature means that changes are frequent, groups go out of existence, contact persons change, and so forth. But this also provides an opportunity for us to make contact with all groups and find out how they are getting on. At the moment we know of 890 groups in the Hamburg area.

ADVISING THOSE INVOLVED IN SELF HELP AND PUTTING THEM IN TOUCH

One of our central tasks is to make it easier for people to gain access to a self help group. We are available on three days a week for eight hours each day (Mondays, Wednesdays and Fridays, 10 a.m. to 4 p.m. and 6 p.m. to 8 p.m.). Interested persons who approach us are informed about self help, in a personal interview, on the telephone or in writing and, if they wish, put in contact with existing groups. If there is no group for the particular concern they are enquiring about, they are put in touch with others who are looking for a group for the same problem or subject. Giving information or putting people in touch through this kind of dialogue often takes a great deal of time, especially when the function of self help groups and the way they run is not clearly understood, so that there is a false expectation of what the Contact and Information Centre is able to do.

In previous years we have been able to make a rough distinction between four groups of enquirers with different needs:

- People who are already well-informed about the principle of self help and are simply looking for a suitable group;
- People who are unclear about the principle of self help and who suppose that we can offer them a therapy, a treatment or a regime;
- People who are in acute need and are seeking help from any institution they can find;
- People who simply want to make contact with someone who will listen to them, who want to pour their heart out to somebody ('Can I ring you again?')

Though this summary is still true of the expectations with which people come to us, we can detect a clear tendency for the first group to increase. We ascribe this to the fact that recent years have seen a great deal of work - much of it carried out by ourselves - to explain what self help groups are, gradually leading to a more realistic idea of the possibilities and limits of self help.

To respond appropriately to these different expectations, we have collected and can make available information about the most important agencies for psychiatric social work and health care in the Hamburg area.

The number of people interested in the work of self

help groups has gone up by leaps and bounds in recent years. In 1983 about 600 people got in touch with us, in 1984 1,400, in 1985 2,600 and in 1986 3,800.

There is a good and bad side to this rapid growth in the number of people involved. It reassures us, of course, about the value of what we are doing; but it also means that we simply have less time and effort available for individuals.

HELP AND SUPPORT IN THE FORM OF ADVICE TO THOSE SETTING UP GROUPS

Advising individuals

When individuals are actively trying to set up a group, we offer advice and help on matters of substance and organization. We discuss together:

where and how potential members of the group can be approached;

the forms of publicity (pamphlets, posters, daily papers, other journals, radio, the Self Help Journal) that can be used to reach the target group;

how and where one can get access to these various types of media;

how and where one can find meeting places, etc.

Besides this we pass on information about the way self help groups work, and about their experiences, we help to make contact with professionals and, if it is necessary and desired, we give support at the initial meeting.

Recently, we have observed a very gratifying development. Increasingly, persons interested in self help are prepared to take the initiative and make an attempt themselves to start a group. Apart from public attitudes which are increasingly sympathetic to self help, the offer of support which the Contact Centre can make plays an essential part. Contact with someone who acts as a colleague seems to be particularly important. In an exhaustive dialogue with the person starting the group, we not only discuss what positive steps have first to be taken to get a group together. We also give encouragement when they still ask with trepidation, 'Can I actually manage this?' We make suggestions about how the work of the group can be structured, and refer them to useful literature. Within this dialogue we also draw attention to frustrations and disappointments that await anyone who starts a group. For example, it is not unusual for a large number of people to respond on the telephone to an advertisement and for very few of them to turn up later at the first meeting. This is all the more disappointing, if the person starting the group has had long, intensive conversations with the callers.

Another problem that must be taken into account is a wide variation in attendance at first. The person who has started the group begins by asking time and again, 'Have I done anything wrong?' They may very well find themselves saying 'I sat all evening and nobody came.' We discuss these possibilities to make it clear that these are things which are not due to personal failure on the part of the person starting the group.

COURSES FOR PEOPLE STARTING GROUPS

For people starting groups who have no experience of them, we have looked at more intensive ways of giving support than can be provided by advice in two or three interviews. We have noticed that people with no experience of groups face almost unsurmountable difficulties when they try to get a self help group going. We therefore offered a course for people starting groups. We regarded the first course as an experiment. It lasted eight weeks, with one meeting a week, and was made up of people who were starting groups, of widely differing ages and for a whole range of problems (multiple sclerosis, phobias, stroke, Recklinghausen's disease, psychoses, eating disorders). The intention of the course was to go beyond what is available in the usual written material and to present typical situations which every group must overcome. Such typical situations are:

the first meeting
getting to know each other better
making rules for the work of the group
getting on with each other
members who join later don't fit in
members don't turn up for meetings
disappointments, conflicts, etc.

All these situations were dealt with in the eight week course. We went to some pains to identify, along with each participant, the dynamics of their groups, and to work out ways in which they might proceed.

Four out of six potential groups came into existence, and three still exist. One came to an end after about a year, one fell apart in the early stages, and one never got going. We plan to continue this form of course for people starting new groups in the future. The disadvantage is that it is very time-consuming. We have therefore considered putting it on at weekends as well, but some of the situations described would possibly not come to the fore in so short a time and therefore could not be used as examples.

CONTINUED SUPPORT IN THE EARLY STAGES

A third possible way of giving groups support in the difficult early stages is to set a time limit on it. This form of more intensive initial support to groups has proved to be particularly useful in the case of groups for eating disorders (anorexia, bulimia, overeating). The indication that this form of support was necessary with these groups was that we had observed several of them collapse in a very short time. The way we deal with this at the moment is to keep a list of the women who call us and then invite them to an initial meeting at which we offer to support the group for a fixed period. During this period we try to show the group ways in which they can give their group a meaningful structure. All the ten groups we supported in this way still exist.

MEETINGS TO SHARE EXPERIENCE

To encourage communication and the exchange of experience between groups we arrange a monthly meeting. It is announced in our Self Help Journal as follows:
'This meeting is for members of self help groups
-   who wish to share their experiences with members of other self help groups
-   who would like to find out whether there are problems in other self help groups and how they have been or are being solved
-   who would like to get to know members of other groups.'
An agenda is not laid down for these meetings. Topics that constantly recur are: How do we cope with new members? Fluctuations in membership. How can we recruit

new members who will get on with us? Crises and conflicts in the group and how to deal with them. How can we work effectively and intensively? What helps the group and what hinders it?

MEETINGS FOR SPECIFIC SPHERES OF INTEREST

Besides the meetings for everyone to share experiences, there are meetings at less regular intervals for specific spheres of interest. Groups are invited to those who are working in the same or in closely related fields and would like to share experience, co-operate or join together. Meetings of this kind have taken place in the following fields: Crohn's disease and colitis ulcerosa groups; pseudo-croup and allergy groups; groups in the psychiatric field; overweight people and women with anorexia, overeating problems and bulimia; groups with forms of cancer.

PUBLICITY

The Self Help Journal

Since 1984 one of the central elements of our publicity work has been the publication of the Self Help Journal. There are five editions a year, each of 5,000-10,000 copies. The purpose of the Journal is to encourage contact between existing groups, to make it easier to start new groups, and to give wide publicity to information about self help. It also gives information about the activities of the Contact Centre. The production, typesetting and layout are as far as possible also a product of self help. The self help groups co-operate in producing and distributing it. The Journal is sent free of charge to all self help groups and to many institutions (counselling centres, doctors, authorities) in Hamburg. A copy is placed in all of the city's fifty public libraries.

'SELF-HELP GROUPS IN HEALTH - THE HAMBURG AREA'

Another important part of our publicity work is this directory which we publish jointly with the Hamburg Health Authority. Six editions have already appeared, and circulation has gone up to 20,000 copies. The directory is made available to all independent medical practitioners in Hamburg, to all hospitals and chemists, and to social service and health service agencies.

COURSES IN PUBLICITY

Since 1985, at the request of many groups, we have begun to organize courses in which self help groups can learn to make use of the tools they need for their own publicity. Since then we have put on three two part courses on the following themes:

Publicity 1: Dealing with the press, radio and television

Publicity 2: How to produce leaflets, pamphlets and newsletters.

These courses have so far been very successful and as time has gone on have become a regular part of the service we offer to groups.

Apart from the activities we have described at length, there are many others we cannot cover in such detail here. For example, with our help a stand for 35 self help groups is organized at a large consumer fair and we put on displays on themes relevant to health, with which we seek to reach a wider public and put the self help idea across to them. And of course even more often we take part in conferences, panel discussions etc., give interviews and talk about our work in the Contact Centre at meetings.

INFORMATION FOR AND CO-OPERATION WITH INTERESTED PROFESSIONALS

The stated aims of the Contact Centre included the following objectives for this part of our work:

We propose to provide training and information sessions for professionals (potential enablers), to inform them of the meaning, mode of operation and effect of self help groups and about the work of the Contact and Information Centre. We hope in this way to ensure professionals co-operate more closely with existing self-help groups, or even encourage new groups to form in their own sphere of work.

We have since made this part of our aim more precise. Because of our very limited staff resources, we have placed the main emphasis of our work on people whose training has a bearing on self help - students and trainees in medicine and psychology, in social work and nursing.

Chapter Nine

LOCAL SUPPORT FOR SELF HELP GROUPS: A FUTURE TASK FOR THE HEALTH, SOCIAL AND EDUCATION SERVICES

Helmut Breitkopf

Based on experience in West Germany, this paper attempts to answer the question of how Self Help Groups (SHG) can be backed up at the local level, over and above the support functions of specially constituted Contact Centres for Self Help. A first step will be to consider the kinds of support which these centres themselves require. These centres provide information and advice and bring together and mediate between the parties involved. It is assumed that the centres have - or should have - an important function in the local Self Help infrastructure, but also that they urgently need the support of institutions and professional personnel from within the health, education and social services. Contact Centres promoting Self Help require support from as many institutions from within the health, social and education services as possible. Assistance is needed in three areas:
- publicity campaigns to spread the idea of Self Help
- provisions of material resources for Self Help
- advice and counselling for individual Groups

I deal first with the role of the Contact Centres and their relations with the services mentioned. Then follows a brief survey of general ways in which the infrastructure of Self Help can receive back-up support from these quarters. I then go on to examine the specialized contributions which could be made by individuals and institutions in these professional fields. I limit myself in this paper to a consideration of the support assistance which could be offered by members of the medical profession, by the National Health Insurance bodies, by charitable organizations, by adult education, by associations for the handicapped and by hospitals.

SUPPORTING THE CONTACT CENTRES

According to the German Working Party on Self Help Groups (DAG SHG) the Contact Centres should have the function of spreading information and mediating between the involved parties.
They aid the contacts:
- between SHG in their local area
- with local authorities and public bodies
- with councillors and local politicians
- with professional bodies and individuals
- with the media
- with the general public

The Contact Centres help the SHG and their members to formulate their requirements and present their arguments to the public. The other way round, they help the SHG to understand the attitudes and interests of the authorities, professionally qualified persons and the general public.

Figure 9.1: The Contact Centre in its information and mediation function

The Public	The Media	Public Authorities	The Political Sphere	Professional Bodies and Institutions

Contact Centres for Self Help Groups

Potential Members of Self Help Groups	Self Help Groups

The various institutions and individuals within the fields of health, education and social services will have different approaches, possibilities and limitations regarding support for Self Help. They can however back up the work of existing Contact Centres and, where possible, lighten the work load of the centres by taking over specific tasks. Apart from their direct involvement with the Contact Centres, there are further ways in which they could offer help and support. These will be considered in the next sections.

GENERAL FORMS OF SUPPORT FROM PUBLIC SERVICES

Institutions and staff members in the official health and social services can help to improve the local infrastructure in various ways. They can:

- provide rooms in the neighbourhood for Self Help Groups and supply materials for group work and publicity
- encourage individuals, whom they meet in the course of their work, to form new SHG in suitable cases and when competent personnel are available
- organize training for workers in the field so as to raise the general level of qualification
- help to create a climate of opinion favourable to Self Help by positive presentation in the media, by publishing information leaflets and giving information talks
- draw attention to the existence of Contact Centres, pass on their information material and encourage interested persons to use their help in getting into touch with a suitable group
- give financial support to Contact Centres and individual SHG

Apart from these general forms of support there are more specialized approaches towards the development of Self Help which could be adopted by specific institutions and professional groups. This will now be examined in more detail.

SPECIALIZED FORMS OF SUPPORT FOR SHG FROM INDIVIDUALS AND INSTITUTIONS WITH THE HEALTH, EDUCATION AND SOCIAL SERVICES

Some of these bodies have their own ideas, plans and activities in the field of Self Help. It is not my purpose to assess these approaches here. My assumption, already stated, is that the Contact Centres have proved to be the most effective instrument for furthering the cause of Self Help and their central function should not be challenged. I am concerned here with outside help of an additional and complementary nature.

SUPPORT FROM MEDICAL PRACTITIONERS

Doctors can give their patients information about SHG and

Contact Centres. They can initiate new Groups in collaboration with the Contact Centres and occasionally step in to help existing groups.

Information can be passed on through leaflets in doctors' waiting rooms and by word of mouth in consultations. The programmes of activities of the Contact Centres could include talks by doctors aimed at encouraging the setting up of SHG. At the very least a medical talk brings together people with the same problem and this is an important first step. Existing SHG may sometimes feel the need for medical information and be pleased to have a doctor present at one of their meetings.

An excellent example of how a doctor can support Self Help is to be found in Lünen-Brambauer, a village on the edge of the Ruhr District. The local Contact Centre originated in a doctor's surgery and has been in existence now for ten years. A local physician, who is also qualified in psychiatry, encouraged his patients - in a way that few other doctors have done - to join together in Self Help groups. In the first few years he more or less did the work of a contact centre. Anyone in the area who is looking for a Self Help Group can enquire at the surgery even if he is not a regular patient. The routine work of the contact centre is now in the hands of voluntary workers from the groups themselves. The role of the doctor is now limited to advising on medical matters and groups' dynamic processes.

Medical practitioners who pass on the idea of SHG to their patients should, however, be aware that a certain motivation and capability on the part of the patient are essential. They also need to check that the groups are ready to welcome new members. Above all, SHG should not be regarded as a way of getting rid of awkward patients. The involvement of doctors in Self Help may mean the rethinking of professional attitudes. Only co-operation between equal partners can ensure that the live character of Self Help is maintained.

SUPPORT FROM HEALTH INSURANCE INSTITUTION EXEMPLIFIED BY THE AOK

The AOK - the General Health Insurance - is the largest health insurance body in West Germany, covering all members of the population who are not eligible for, or do not wish to join more specialized insurance schemes. It has

the broadest network of local branches and has started recently to take an interest in Community health care activities.
In the way of support for SHG, the AOK could:
- inform their members (insured persons) about the work of the Contact Centres
- perform at least some of the functions of a Contact Centre in places where these do not exist
- undertake a form of sponsorship for individual SHG
- support Contact Centres and SHG with money and materials
- allow Self Help organizations to use their office facilities.

The AOK is well placed to carry out these tasks through its existing counselling service, which is offered to any member needing advice on any health related topic. In appropriate cases, the clients are passed on to specialized institutions, such as marriage guidance, family planning centres, drug addiction counsellors - and Contact Centres for Self Help. Only when such institutions are lacking in the local area, does the counselling service fill the gap itself.

The AOK for the Mettmann District has been maintaining five Contact and Information Centres for Self Help as a pilot project since 1984. They are run in connection with the local Health Centres in this rural district.

The health insurance bodies have a specially important role, where SHG need regular financial support. This could arise, for instance, when a Rheumatism Group wants to do weekly exercises in warm water. The Health Insurance could help to carry the costs and, just as important, help with the necessary administrative procedures.

There are also examples of health insurance bodies supporting individual SHG. In general in the Federal Republic the AOK gives financial and practical help to rheumatism sufferers. Other official health insurances have taken on the sponsorship of SHG.

The usefulness of the health insurances to Self Help is, however, restricted by the fact that each insurance can only give direct support to its own members, which means that a SHG may have to approach a different insurance, with different policies. Furthermore, the insurances, though state backed, are in competition with each other. This competition is very intense at present and means that the AOK, for example, is forced to exploit its commitment to

Self Help in the 'market place', which can have unfavourable effects on day to day collaboration.

SUPPORT FROM CHARITIES, EXEMPLIFIED BY THE DPWV

The DPWV - the German Equitable Welfare Association - is one of six large combined charitable associations in West Germany and has over 4,000 member organizations, including self help organizations for the handicapped. Affiliation to the DPWV is open to all charities of a non-political, non-confessional character. For this reason and because of its traditional ties with the handicapped, the DPWV has a positive attitude to helping Self Help. Specifically, the Association is in a position to provide rooms and office facilities for Contact Centres and SHG, as a so-called 'Resource Pool'. In addition, it can spread the idea of Self Help through its affiliated organizations for the handicapped. Finally, SHG which develop in the direction of wanting a more permanent organizational structure, perhaps in order to set up and administer their own institutional facilities may find it useful to become formal members of the DPWV.

Recent developments indicate that the association is coming to see the increased promotion of Self Help as a central task. In some towns in Germany there are Contact Centres directly founded and run by the DPWV or receiving support through membership of the association.

As a rule, however, SHG do not want or need to be closely tied to charitable associations. Problems can sometimes arise from the fact that powerful organizations like the DPWV can exert a kind of 'magnetic pull' on their co-operation partner, who may feel in danger of being taken over.

SUPPORT FROM ADULT EDUCATION

Adult Education Centres are specially well equipped to:
- assist the Contact Centres in starting up new SHG
- help the work of existing SHG by running courses and classes on health topics
- offer special training for persons involved in developing Self Help

Initiating SHG by means of adult education classes

requires a special planning concept which still has to be worked out. As a first step, the idea of Self Help must be given an important place in health education generally. Contact with students can be maintained after a class or course is finished and their interest in Self Help encouraged. An Adult Education Centre can let SHG use its rooms from time to time and can set up new classes to meet their special needs in fields like gymnastics and diet. Appropriate training courses can be offered to staff from the social and health services who are inexperienced in the techniques of Self Help. It is also necessary to give in-service training to adult education tutors in the health field, in view of their important role in initiating Self Help. The potential of adult education in helping to initiate SHG is being tested at present in the College of Adult Education in Unna. With the co-operation of the tutors, the students in classes and lectures on health topics are made aware of the idea of Self Help. At the end of the course further meetings are arranged and technical and organizational help is provided for those who are interested in going together to form groups.

SUPPORT FROM ASSOCIATIONS FOR THE HANDICAPPED

There are over forty associations for the handicapped in West Germany at present. They try to help their members come to terms with their disabilities and offer them a wide range of personal services. They also act as political pressure groups. As a rule they are registered as non-profit making institutions and are organized in a hierarchical structure of local groups, state and federal associations. The handicapped individual tends to regard them as a source of outside assistance rather than as a means of Self Help. By working together with Contact Centres, the handicapped organizations could, however, play a part in stimulating Self Help, which would meet their members' needs for active contact with fellow sufferers and mutual support and encouragement. The handicapped association have their own publications which could propagate and encourage the idea of Self Help.

More active support in future for the formation of small local SHG within the handicapped organization is also strongly recommended by the National Federation of Aid for the Handicapped, which represents a number of national organizations. It is especially recommended that organizational help should be given to groups whose members provide their own services on the basis of mutual assistance.

SUPPORT FROM HOSPITALS AND CLINICS

The particular forms of support which hospitals can offer are:
- encouraging a positive attitude to Self Help on the part of patients and their families
- helping to initiate new SHG
- bringing patients into contact with suitable SHG seeking new members

All these activities can be best carried out in close co-operation with a local Contact Centre. The Contact Centres will keep the hospitals informed about the work of existing SHG and supply a whole range of other information. Hospitals and clinics can help the initiation of new Groups by putting rooms at the disposal of patients who want to talk about their experiences and exchange ideas, by inviting SHG to come and describe their activities and by encouraging individual patients to found new Groups with the help of the Contact Centres. Hospitals can play an especially valuable role in stimulating Self Help among patients' families. There are cases where hospital staff have helped to set up Groups for the relatives of emotionally disturbed patients, for the parents of children with cancer and for members of families facing the problems of bereavement.

A cancer clinic in Hamburg tries to familiarize its patients with the idea of Self Help already during the period of medical treatment. After the treatment the hospital social workers co-operate with Cancer Self Help organizations, trying to encourage ex-patients to form groups or to start new groups.

Hospitals and clinics which want to support Self Help may need minor modifications to their facilities, but the main requirement is for suitable qualified staff. In the long term, the techniques of Self Help support should be included in the normal training of doctors and other medical staff. In addition in-service training could be organized within the hospital.

SUMMARY

This paper attempted to describe the specific ways in which institutions, professional groups and individuals from within the fields of social welfare, health and education can make a contribution to supporting Self Help. It was a basic assumption that the central stimulus and comprehensive back-up services can only come from truly independent Self Help Contact Centres, which are open to all sections of the population. The medical profession, the health administration, educational institutions and other bodies cannot achieve this. They have their own aims and interests which can make it difficult for them to support Self Help purely for its own sake. Furthermore each institution only has dealings with a limited section of the public. Nevertheless, these institutions can make their own valuable contribution alongside and in co-operation with the Contact Centres. They can facilitate the setting up of new Groups and support the day-to-day activities of existing groups. Doctors can inform their patients about SHG and encourage participation. They can advise and inform Groups about medical matters. Health insurances can look after individual groups, taking a form of sponsorship. They can help with office work and administration.

Charitable organizations can take under their wing those Groups which develop a tighter organization and want to move into regular health care activities.

Educational institutions are well placed to offer appropriate training courses for persons working with SHG. Their health education classes can be a starting point for the emergence of new Groups.

Organizations for the handicapped can extend their function as service organizations and pressure groups and respond to their members' needs for mutual support and a more active role.

Hospitals can help Self Help by passing on information and advice to their patients and also to their families. They can especially help to ensure that interested persons get into contact with Self Help at an early stage in their case history.

The support of the organizations and professional groups mentioned in this paper could be very significant for the 'Future of Self Help' and it is to be hoped that they will come to see this as a worthwhile subsidiary task alongside the main work. It is, however, highly desirable that all these support activities should be co-ordinated, and therefore the setting up of independent Contact Centres for Self Help in every town and country district remains a first priority.

The benefits for the institutions and individuals of the Health and Social Services which involve themselves in Self Help are not simply that doctors have more contented patients or that insurance and welfare associations gain more members. An involvement with Self Help can lead persons and professional bodies to an increased awareness of the limitations of traditional institutionalized services and perhaps bring about a change in attitudes regarding their vocational roles. If this happens, it is perhaps legitimate to hope that Self Help Groups will receive from these sources the technical and financial help, the professional advice and support, all in the right place, which they need in order to overcome their common problems.

Chapter Ten

ENGLISH SELF HELP SUPPORT IN CONTEXT

Judith Unell

The papers by Judy Wilson and Judith Unell in this section of the report consider some aspects of the English experience of community development work with self help groups. Both papers draw heavily upon the authors' involvement with a single pioneering project, the Nottingham Self Help Team.

The Self Help Team is the longest-established local self help support centre in England and at the beginning of our series of seminars it was the only one which could present results of systematic monitoring and evaluation. Happily, the past three years have seen a sudden increase in self help support. It has attracted more resources, more activity and more attention. The small band of self help support workers of 1984 has become a flourishing national network; central government has backed an awakening interest in self help with a modest funding programme for local support work; and a national clearing house, The National Self Help Support Centre, has been set up in response to local demands for information, training and the opportunity to share experience in working with self help groups. These developments need to be more fully explained if the international reader is to understand the context within which local support centres are now working.

Providing support for self help is not an activity which has been discovered recently in England. The 1960s and 1970s saw the birth of many new national voluntary organizations, based upon specific social issues such as poverty, homelessness and single parenthood. They were concerned to publicize and promote the interests of their members as 'consumers' rather than as passive recipients of services. Some encouraged the development of a network of local groups with both campaigning and mutual support functions, usually affiliated to the national body and receiving support and information from it. Over the same period, several large and well-known organizations serving 'traditional' client groups such as deaf, physically disabled and mentally handicapped people modified paternalistic attitudes and developed new patterns of service delivery and client advocacy. The client was to be given a new voice within the organization, and local member groups were to be acknowledged as a vital channel for allowing that voice to be heard.

The mutual support functions of local groups were given a new emphasis alongside their more traditional tasks of fundraising and providing services. A rearranging of attitudes within the established voluntary sector was accompanied by efforts to make management structures more widely representative by including more sufferers and carers. Some organizations changed their names at this time in order to reflect their commitment to work as partners to those in need.

A recognition of the value of self help and a desire to encourage it by providing appropriate support are, therefore, important themes in the recent history of voluntary action in England. The emphasis has been on support provided at national or regional levels to affiliated groups of specialist organizations. (1) Much newer is the growth of local centres of support which are generalist in their approach, supporting groups which are very different from each other in their problems and concerns. The development of such centres has depended upon the readiness of community development workers and of groups themselves to make an imaginative leap across the barrier erected around a particular 'problem' or 'condition' towards an understanding of self help as a process which has common features within groups with very different motivating problems. A small number of projects and services have been influential in demonstrating the effectiveness of generalist support.

The Self Help Team has played a particularly important part. It grew out of the community work of a voluntary development agency in Nottingham whose staff in the late 1970s began to identify a number of groups which had been established to provide mutual support and solidarity for people suffering from common health problems. When sporadic work in supporting such groups matured and coalesced in 1982 into a special self help support project, there was immediate interest in its progress among staff in voluntary organizations and also professional workers in statutory health and welfare agencies in many parts of the country, indicating a general awareness of the growth of self help and a widespread desire to encourage it further.

Supporting self help came to be seen as an activity which could be distinguished from general community development work and The Self Help Team was not alone in attracting attention to the growth of self help groups and their need for support and resources. A pioneering information exchange, 'Help for Health', had been established in a health authority in the south of England in 1980 to improve access to information for patients, people providing informal care for sick or dependent individuals in their homes and neighbourhoods, and health care staff. It collects and disseminates health care information and details of self help groups and voluntary organizations. The service is regionally based but has attracted enquiries from all parts of the country and its innovative approach has influenced national thinking on how to provide information for self care and self help.

By 1984, there was a tiny handful of new projects whose main task was to provide support for self help. A Self Help Groups Project had been established in Leicester with funding from the local authority, and a voluntary mental health organization had set up a support centre for self help groups with a mental health focus within two London boroughs. Projects specializing in self help support were slow to emerge but many local voluntary organizations and statutory bodies, notably social services departments, were now offering support to self help as part of a wider community development task. An informal contact network developed between workers who were supporting self help in a variety of settings and this gave rise to the first meeting of the Self Help National Network in September 1984.

THE SELF HELP NATIONAL NETWORK (2)

The Self Help National Network holds an annual meeting of workers and researchers who are engaged in work with self help groups in a local setting. The first two Network meetings were organized by workers themselves but the National Self Help Support Centre has now taken on this task and provides information back-up. The Network has been strengthened by this injection of support and by the impetus given to the funding of local projects by the Self Help Alliance (see below). Numbers attending the annual meetings have risen sharply each year, from 20 in 1984 to over 100 at the most recent meeting in 1987. Changing venues have helped to draw individuals and organizations from all parts of the country into the Network; for example, the 1987 meeting in Newcastle was well supported by workers in the North-East and Scotland.

The meetings have given support workers an opportunity to share their particular experiences of supporting self help in very different localities and to exchange ideas about aspects of support such as setting up an information service or providing training opportunities for group members.

In this way the National Network has contributed to the growth of good practice. It has also provided a forum for members to discuss general issues which arise from their work. Several key themes have recurred, reflecting the common preoccupations of support workers.

There has been much debate about the problems of defining self help groups. In practice, self help tends to shade off into other kinds of activity, and workers have, on the one hand, needed to impose some boundaries around their work while at the same time recognizing that their own definitions of self help may not be shared by the groups they serve.

Finding constructive ways of working with professional workers in the context of self help support has been another important talking point. Support workers have been divided between their desire to enable professional workers in the statutory health and social welfare services to provide effective support for groups and their fears that groups will thereby be incorporated into the professional repertoire as a low-cost means of administering and delivering services.

A similar ambivalence has been expressed about the involvement of central government in funding self help support. There have been practical objections to the government's now well-established practice of launching short-term initiatives to fund work on long-term problems in local areas. But, at a deeper level, doubts have been expressed about the motivations of government in stimulating support for self help. Is it simply recognizing that self help is a valuable dimension of health and social care which needs more space to develop or does it perhaps see self help as a component to be built into low-cost programmes of community care which may undermine professional services?

With the launch of a new funding strategy for self help support in 1984, these questions were no longer theoretical. By that time, however, the voluntary sector in England had learned important lessons about how to respond to short-term government funding opportunities in order to maximize the benefits for voluntary action and to minimize some of the inherent dangers. In particular, the usefulness of creating consortia and networks of national voluntary bodies to administer temporary government programmes had been demonstrated. A new consortium now came into being around the issue of self help support.

THE SELF HELP ALLIANCE (3)

In 1984, central government, through the Department of Health and Social Security, launched an initiative called 'Helping the Community to Care'. Provision for funding local work in supporting self help was included in the three-year programme and eighteen local self help support projects had been established by the early months of 1986.

Responsibility for overseeing the development of the projects and providing central support was delegated to a consortium of national voluntary organizations, The Self Help Alliance. Researchers from the Tavistock Institute undertook the evaluation of the scheme under the joint management of the DHSS and the Alliance. These arrangements helped to disarm suspicions of extensive government interference in the deployment of resources. It also enabled the voluntary sector to make a coherent contribution to the design of the self help initiative in its early stages. The Alliance was given complete authority over the process of grant allocation and the selection of projects from bids received. Each applicant was required to provide evidence of support from local self help groups and from local health authorities and social services departments. Less than one third of the voluntary organizations which submitted firm bids received funding under the programme, an indication of the widespread interest in self help support within the local voluntary sector. Also, the Alliance was concerned to provide adequate levels of funding for each project rather than disperse the available resources widely but in small amounts. Most projects were funded over a three year period at a level sufficient to meet their running expenses and the costs of employing up to two full-time workers.

Grant aid has been directed mainly to projects managed by councils for voluntary service which coordinate and develop voluntary action at local level in most areas of England. There are a few examples of less orthodox host agencies such as a women's mental health collective and a community book shop. However, the Alliance failed to reach some groups which operate outside the established voluntary sector networks. In particular, there were few good applications from black-managed organizations, although some of the funded projects have a specific brief to work with ethnic minority groups. This reveals an important weakness of a funding strategy which filters money to local groups through coherent national networks of voluntary organizations. Those who do not belong to a network may be left out.

The continuing monitoring and evaluation of the Alliance projects will yield important information about the development of self help support. These findings are not yet available but interim reports submitted by the projects to the Alliance during the first six months of the scheme suggested that the development of new self help groups through the direct support of group leaders was a core activity for most projects. Information resource work was an important adjunct to group work although projects differed in the scale of their activities in this area. Some had access to computers and/or additional part-time information workers while others were accumulating information in a more sporadic way.

The provision of training opportunities is another shared concern. Some projects had set up their own training events and others were encouraging other local organizations to provide suitable training for self help group members.

This latter approach reflects a widespread readiness to form partnerships with a range of local voluntary and statutory bodies in order to shift their attitudes and practices towards self help support. Clearly, the Alliance projects have not confined themselves to providing direct services to self help groups in their areas. Most are working to create a climate within the local voluntary and statutory sectors which is more receptive to the needs of self help groups.

The opportunity to link with other projects with a similar focus in order to share problems, compare progress and participate in joint training events has been an important advantage for workers within the Alliance programme. A central unit with two paid staff has co-ordinated shared activities and disseminated information to projects; also, the Tavistock Institute has provided a programme of joint evaluation workshops. However, care has been taken to avoid the creation of an exclusive worker group within the area of self help support. The Self Help National Network draws together all projects into a national forum and the recently established National Self Help Support Centre provides a focus for self help support which transcends regional and programme boundaries and which will continue when the central unit of the Alliance closes at the end of the three-year national funding period.

THE NATIONAL SELF HELP SUPPORT CENTRE

The National Self Help Support Centre is an independent initiative sponsored by two major national voluntary organizations, the Volunteer Centre and the National Council for Voluntary Organizations. It was set up in January 1986 with funding from charitable sources. Two part-time workers are employed, a development worker and an assistant.

The activities of the Centre echo the work of local self help support projects. It has a promotional role, working to increase awareness of self help and of the importance of support for self help at the national level. It provides support and information to local workers engaged in self help support. The circulation of a quarterly news bulletin is part of this task and a directory of local self help support projects has been produced. Further publications on self help are also planned. The linking together of local workers is another concern and the Centre now administers the Self Help National Network. In addition, it has organized a network of Black workers, and there have been moves to bring together workers in national organizations who have a brief to support local branches or groups. The Centre is concerned to improve the quality and quantity of training available to support workers and self help group members by piloting training materials and organizing a programme of training events.

<u>So far so good.</u>

Self help support has developed rapidly in England over the past three years from very small beginnings. It must be said that the scale of support work, both locally and nationally, remains modest and self help is of marginal concern to most service providers. But at this stage it is perhaps more important that the right framework exists to enable self help to grow.

National organizations and pioneering local projects have offered good demonstrations of how to provide appropriate support and this work has captured widespread attention within the voluntary sector and in government. The evaluation of the projects funded through the Self Help Alliance will be a valuable addition to our knowledge about development work with self help groups. Government funding of local support work has been a spur to action within the voluntary sector and effective management of the programme by national voluntary organizations has alleviated many (but not all) anxieties about government involvement in this area. The Self Help National Network has become a regular forum for growing numbers of local and national support workers and the National Self Help Support Centre will help to sustain and improve their work by offering better information and training and by promoting awareness of self help.

Local self help support in England commands a great deal of energy and commitment and it now has a sound structure. It remains to be seen whether the impetus provided by central government can be sustained when its funding programme ceases. In the ideal future, the promotion of self-help at the local level would be guaranteed by permanent local sources of funding for development work. But, as in most areas of voluntary sector activity in England at present, there is a great deal of hope and very little certainty.

NOTES

1.   For a research-based account of local self help activity in four national voluntary organizations see Richardson A. and Goodman M. Self Help and Social Care: Mutual Aid Organizations in Practice. Policy Studies Institute, 1983.

2.   This section has drawn upon reports of the annual meetings of the Self Help Network. Copies of the reports are available from Mai Wann, National Self Help Support Centre, 26 Bedford Square, London WC1 (tel: 01-636-4066).

3.   Darvill, G., Self Help Alliance: Activities in Projects, April to September 1986. Self Help Alliance internal paper, October 1986.

For a more detailed account of the government funding programme for local self help support see Darvill, G., Self Help initiatives put DHSS funds to good use, Social Services Insight, 9-16 August 1986.

Chapter Eleven

FROM PHILOSOPHY TO PARTNERSHIP

Judy Wilson

Self help may not be new, but the idea of clearing houses - locally provided support for self help groups - is comparatively recent. Clearing houses are not predictable organizations. They have felt their way cautiously, responded to local needs, changed as people reacted to their services. This caution, responsiveness and variety have been their strengths. One cannot say when working with self help groups: 'These are the services you need, use them.' But cautiousness can also lead to lack of confidence, and the loss of opportunities for useful action.

The time would seem ripe, in both Germany and the UK, for a greater degree of confidence in the work of clearing houses, their philosophy and their potential influence on other local agencies. Let us pose some questions. What can clearing houses do - and do well? What might be their philosophy? What local agencies might they work with and how might they influence them? And, finally, what implications are there for their work?

PHILOSOPHY AND PRACTICE

One must be brave to put forward ideas on philosophy and practice for each local clearing house, as experience has shown, will evolve its own. There are now in the UK and in Germany annual meetings of clearing houses, and a national clearing house to organize them but there is no recognized structure, nor a national set-up which imposes rules and regulations. It is significant that at a meeting held in Leuven in early 1986 representatives of clearing houses

128

threw out the idea of a model, a blueprint. (1) If, however, one does not look for common elements in beliefs and work, opportunities for understanding and furthering work of this comparatively recent type of organization may be lost, and newcomers will not be able to draw on the experience of those longer in the field. Experience of bringing clearing houses together shows there is a common core of understanding. As long as one does not attempt to impose ideas on them, then it is actually constructive to put forward ideas on what might be their philosophy and practice.

The ultimate goal of clearing houses, I would suggest, should be to help self help groups realize their own aims. Associated with this should be a philosophy of enabling rather than promoting new developments; of introducing people to each other rather than co-ordinating them; of accepting that self help group members themselves decide on their work and structure, on whether they use the clearing house and whether they will co-operate with the outside world. From a more practically orientated angle, clearing houses should work from a standpoint of involving local self help groups in their policy and priorities, but being realistic about the degree to which this is practicable. They should constantly monitor, get feedback, evaluate and change their services. They should start from a basis of not knowing what end results there will be of their work. At the root of their work, lastly, is a belief in empowerment, but the degree to which this is explicit - or indeed shared with funders - must depend on local circumstances.

It is easier to list the practical tasks that local clearing houses might undertake. Discussions at Leuven, and earlier might undertake. Discussions at Leuven, and earlier at Hohr-Grenzhausen (2) brought together lists of services that were generally agreed as useful and needed. Here one can only summarize their main functions:
- the collection and dissemination of information
- practical back-up services (e.g. money, rooms, typing, literature)
- help with new groups and problem-solving in established groups
- provision of 'training' and the means of groups meeting each other
- work with professionals, the media and local and health authorities.

While each clearing house will select its own priorities,

we should now feel confident that this type of work is important, used and valued - and fills a gap that no one else will fill. If this is so, can and indeed should, local support centres of this kind work with other local agencies? And on what basis might they do so?

CLEARING HOUSES AS INFLUENCERS

We have a dilemma. On the one hand it would seem right for clearing houses to take up and seek opportunities to influence other agencies so acting on behalf of self help groups. On the other hand workers are not elected representatives with a mandate to speak and self help groups are so disparate, one might question if it is possible to generalize about their needs. The conclusion of workers meeting in Leuven was that the extensive use of clearing houses by groups legitimates their role. Clearing houses, as concerned friends, closely in touch with groups, can take up opportunities to influence practice and extend the availability of resources in other local agencies.

WORK WITH PROFESSIONALS

Let us look at some examples of work by the Nottingham Self Help Team, first at work with local professionals and then at partnership with two particular local agencies. Work with new groups proved from the beginning, in 1982, to be an important part of the work of the Team. Much of the work was done by the Team itself, but in some cases its role was to work with a local health or social service professional who was the key person in enabling the growth of a group. How successful was this? One can look at the question of success in two ways. Did the clearing house succeed in getting professionals to listen, think and amend their practice in a way in which it was thought was needed? And did self running self help groups emerge from their work? In over half the cases, the answer to both was yes. Much seems to depend on the outlook and personal characteristics of individuals. Where it was flexible and informal - people who one can call 'instinctive enablers' - professionals seemed able to step aside from their normal role, without any loss of status when operating within it, and successfully work with self help groups. Where people were very traditional and formal about their role with clients and patients, and insistent upon a particular form of organization, the likelihood of them either working co-operatively with the clearing house, or a self running group emerging, was remote.

The actual amount of time spent with the instinctive enablers was often brief, but the amount of influence high. More time was spent with a third category, the 'enablers in principle'. If it was possible to allocate substantial time, and to co-operate over a lengthy period (maybe 6 months to a year) then the clearing house appeared to be influential and the likelihood of a group emerging greater. Brief conversations, however, left workers feeling, as one said, 'confused'.

A longer term piece of work was undertaken with the medical school. Since 1983 a regular seminar has been held six times a year, run jointly by a general practitioner attached to the medical school, the team leader and a succession of local self help groups. Initial reaction from the students, through a questionnaire, was one of interest and willingness to learn about groups. While the long term results of this are not known, the partnership of the local G.P. and the Self Help Team undoubtedly influenced the medical school to give up time in a pressured syllabus, and to continue this on a regular basis for four years. As a seed sowing exercise it was successful.

HEALTH EDUCATION UNIT

Nottingham Health Authority is unusual in having a forward looking health education unit. The amount of interaction between it and the Self Help Team has been variable, but the degree of common outlook was considerable. The relationship began with a request for a substantial piece of help from the team, to do the artwork and layout of a starter pack for new groups without charge, which proved to be a successful piece of partnership.

Other pieces of co-operation followed. Two particular groups, the Stop Smoking group and the Positive Health group, got substantial help and back-up from staff of the unit without members losing control of the group. New workers in the unit were appointed on a neighbourhood basis to work with a range of community health initiatives, employed by the unit but coming to have quite close co-operation with the team. An attempt to publicly further the links between groups and the unit failed, however, when a jointly organized public meeting attracted very few people from groups.

The trigger for co-operation was the presence of a member of the unit on the team's advisory group, but the personal interest of the Head of the unit undoubtedly made the partnership possible and flexible. And the degree of common philosophy, based on a concept of people contributing to their own health, was considerable. It is, again, difficult to qualify the extent of the Self Help Team's influence on the unit, but it undoubtedly came to provide increased resources and services to benefit self help groups.

COMMUNITY RADIO TEAM

Local radio has proved in the UK to be a valuable source of information about self help groups, but as with other forms of the media, brings risks of journalists using them for their own ends. There are examples of groups being harmed rather than helped by local radio stations. And it can be the groups who are confident, well-resourced and perhaps better able to sell themselves in other ways who get air time. The opportunity to influence and co-operate with the two local radio stations came in 1983, when a community radio team was established. Like the Self Help Team it was managed by the Nottingham Council for Voluntary Service, so co-operation was immediate and easy. It took a variety of forms:
- provision of information about groups to the radio team
- joint production of a booklet, 'Using Local Radio'
- jointly organized training
- linking new groups with both teams
- challenging the bad practice of some radio team workers.

Here the Self Help Team, already well established, was working with a group of enthusiastic and mainly young workers, some committed to the self help group approach and staying in post some time, others not. The importance of the Radio Team was as intermediary with the radio stations, and its work undoubtedly led to more air time for groups, back-up facilities and material for broadcasts and greater visibility and tacit approval of the self help idea. The role of the Self Help team was to back up their work, challenge it constructively and to increase the links groups had with them. The degree of common philosophy was high, aided by the personal involvement of the first radio worker with a self help group, and a shared belief in people doing things for themselves.

AN ANALYSIS OF ROLES AND INFLUENCE

Let us look at the varying roles played by the Self Help Team in all three areas of work. One can group them as:

> protector of self help groups
> information provider and updater
> interpreter of groups
> trainer
> campaigner for resources

None of this work was planned at the outset in detail. It came about either because people approached the team for help, or the team perceived opportunities for influence and partnership and took them.

How successful was it? In some cases, such as the medical students, one cannot predict change - one can only sow seeds and hope. In other cases, the amount of interaction and influence was high. The key ingredients would seem to be, first, a shared philosophy of what self help groups were about, and the role of outsiders with them. Second, while it was important that the agency was generally sympathetic to shared work with the Self Help Team, more significant was the personal outlook and degree of flexibility and sensitivity of individuals within it. Third, for there to be success there needed to be a mixture of practical co-operation and the possibility of a substantial allocation of time for discussion, planning and support. In conclusion, bearing in mind the small size of the Self Help Team, where these ingredients were present the degree of its influence was considerable.

IMPLICATIONS FOR THE WORK OF THE CLEARING HOUSES

Clearing houses, as has been outlined, benefit from a worked out philosophy to help their own work. What is now seen is that this can also aid the identification of allies and partners with whom work can be done. For it is alliances, largely informal, that have proved to be the way forward. Clearing houses are not powerful organizations, they cannot exert influence on other people's practice from a power base. It only comes through co-operation and mutually helpful pieces of work.

Time is a problem. Only clearing houses with paid staff will be able to undertake the sort of work described here, and even then they will be constantly battling with demands of all sorts on their limited time. Alliances can only work with substantial investment of time; back-up information requires an efficiently run information service; individuals need time to discuss, change and experiment. And it is not only actual hours in the week. This way of working requires too continuity of relationships, and hence continuity of staffing and funding of clearing houses.

In a town of any size, the number of potential allies may be great, but there will be a large variety in their outlook and commitment to self help. The way forward would seem to be to concentrate on situations where it is likely there will be success and co-operation, and not to batter on closed doors.

But opportunities must be seized. Clearing houses are rarely large - and in fact a big staff can be a disadvantage. Their work can be enhanced and extended through a ripple effect out from their basic work to other agencies. I began by urging clearing houses to feel confident about their role and philosophy. I will end by encouraging them to feel further confidence in their ability to influence and work with other agencies who can also help self help groups realize their own aims.

Finally, let us not underestimate the challenge of this way of working. It is a precarious role and one which one cannot always be too public about. Often it is background work which counts. One local clearing house working alone may find it difficult to sustain such an approach. What are needed are opportunities to share and discuss with colleagues in other clearing houses elsewhere to avoid isolation and to identify and promote good practice.

NOTES

1. Supporting Self Help Groups. Report of a

workshop held at Leuven, Belgium, January 1986.
  2.   From Research to Supportive Policy. Report of a
workshop held at Hohr Grenzhausen, Germany, June 1982.

Chapter Twelve

LOCAL SUPPORT FOR SELF HELP. MORE DIFFICULT THAN IT LOOKS?

Judith Unell

Local support for self help in England and West Germany is strongly rooted in a community development tradition. Out of this tradition has emerged a set of organizing principles which are widely acknowledged and shared by self help support workers. (1) This short paper looks at some of the dilemmas which may arise for workers as they try to interpret their day-to-day work with self help groups in the light of these accepted norms. The paper draws upon a research study of the Nottingham Self Help Team. The dilemmas faced by the Team were, of course, prompted by unique local circumstances and yet, at another level, they illustrate tensions which may be encountered within any local support centre.

THE COMMON ELEMENTS

The common areas of agreement between self help support workers seem to be that:
- Support centres should be responsive in their orientation to self help groups. They should not be in the business of recruiting leaders for groups or actively organizing them in other ways. The need for a new group should have been identified within the local community. The task of the support centre is to work in partnership with lay people who have seen a need and who wish to respond by developing a self help group.
- Support centres should be enabling rather than directive. As Judy Wilson suggests in her paper, this means a philosophy of 'introducing people to each other rather than

co-ordinating them; of accepting that self help group members themselves decide on their work and structure'. Support workers are seen as discreet providers of advice and resources rather than forthright prescribers. The aim is to nurture groups towards independence. This in turn implies that workers sometimes need to place limits upon the length and amount of their involvement with groups.

\- Support centres should seek to protect groups from destructive and unwelcome pressures. Pressure can be exerted from various directions. Governments, both local and central, may seek to manipulate groups for their own cost-saving and service-delivery ends. Professional workers may have the effect, often unwittingly, of subverting the confidence and independence of groups. National organizations to which local groups are affiliated are sometimes tempted to regard local self help groups as a means of raising more money and adding to their prestige. Support workers appear to accept the need for a protective role in such cases but are often ambivalent about assuming a more open campaigning stance.

\- Support centres should sustain the independence of self help groups. This principle is embedded in the other principles already outlined. It also has implications for the practical support of local groups. Many support centres provide basic administrative backing and perhaps a meeting place for local groups but feel that they should not encourage dependency by providing a comprehensive servicing system.

THE PRACTICAL DILEMMAS

Despite this relatively coherent view of the role of the local support centre, some interesting dilemmas may arise in the day-to-day existence of support workers who face a multiplicity of demands with characteristically small budgets and limited time. Also, the injunction to respond and enable may present workers with difficult choices and place unforeseen limits upon the scope of the centre's work.

THE LIMITS OF RESPONSIVENESS

A responsive orientation is convenient as well as appropriate for most local self help support centres. Not only does it fit

137

well with a non-interventionist style but it provides a
mechanism for limiting the workload. Help is given to those
who come forward to seek it. Support workers will usually
draw back from evangelizing for self help among members
of the community who show little spontaneous interest in
this approach and most would hesitate before trying to
initiate a new group without the promise of local
involvement and leadership.

The strategy may well be a rational one for a self help
support centre which requires a manageable workload and
well-defined aims in order to perform effectively.
However, an important consequence which needs to be
recognized is that the impact of the support centre may
then be confined to a relatively limited segment of the
community.

Most English self-help support centres (and these are
still few in number and relatively recent) have been created
by established voluntary bodies which function as
community development agencies in their localities.
Although these 'intermediary bodies' are becoming
increasingly aware of the need to adapt their work to serve
minorities, particularly black people, most will still be seen
as representing the interests of vocal and established white
groups. A support centre is likely to share the constituency
of its 'host' agency. It may well lack the inside knowledge
which is necessary to work effectively and harmoniously
with minority communities. It also risks being perceived as
alien by their members.

The Nottingham Self Help Team received very few
requests for help from black people, and local network
meetings of self help groups attracted almost no black
participants. This points to the need for new strategies for
promoting and explaining the work of a support centre
among ethnic minorities. But the gap cannot necessarily be
bridged by better information alone. A deeper understanding
by support workers of the meaning of self help and self care
within other cultures is also needed. It is likely that many
people who place a high value on mutual support do not
organize this support around specific health conditions or
problems. Their health care needs may not be framed in a
way which makes them readily intelligible to a support
centre with a problem-centred approach.

Other groups will have different problems in finding
support for self help. A support centre which is based within
the central area of a city or town could prove inaccessible

to people from housing developments in outlying areas. Over the period covered by the research, the Nottingham Self Help Team was rather unsuccessful in supporting isolated neighbourhood groups based outside the city centre. Elderly people appear to use self help infrequently as a mechanism for coping. Bedridden patients and mentally handicapped people are examples of other groups who lack the mobility or the capacity for self expression which membership of a group demands.

Many other cultural, geographical and personal barriers to the development of self help could no doubt be highlighted. A support centre with a 'responsive' orientation must work within the limits which they impose. But do these limits matter? After all a self help support centre is already serving people who are deprived and disadvantaged by their health and social problems. Is it not more important to carry out a limited task effectively than to try to make self help relevant to all groups within the population?

Most support workers will recognize that limited time and resources demand a realistic work programme but will also be aware that a demand-led approach risks concentrating resources too narrowly among groups in the community which are already 'tuned in' to self help and self care. Distributing scarce support more equitably is a real concern. There is not yet enough systematic evidence about support to self help in England to assess whether self help support centres are successfully building bridges to the black community (although the Alliance programme does include projects with a special emphasis upon work with ethnic minorities). However, there are indications, both in England and other countries, that support workers recognize the need for experimental styles of developing new groups which can make self help accessible to more people. One approach has been to offer people with a common problem a structured introduction to the experience of meeting in a group.

This approach was successfully adopted by the Nottingham Self Help Team in partnership with social workers at a local hospital in order to launch a support group for infertile couples. Previous attempts to develop a group within the hospital had been opposed by some medical staff and had aroused little apparent interest among patients, despite evidence that many infertile couples need continuing support and information. It was decided to organize an open series of talks and discussions on infertility in an independent setting. Towards the end of the course the idea of starting a self help group was suggested to the participants and promptly taken up. At this point the social workers withdrew and the Self Help Team continued to support the new group.

This is reminiscent of the style of working described by some of our German colleagues who have successfully introduced the suggestion of creating a self help group to people attending for treatment in a clinic or following an educational course concerned with a specific health problem. The assumption is that people who could benefit from participation in a self help group are not always aware of its potential and may not have the confidence to put themselves forward to lead a group.

The work of the New Jersey clearing house in the USA (2) also demonstrates the possibility of a more assertive approach in initiating new groups. People who call to enquire about the availability of a group for their own problem and who discover that none exists will be offered the opportunity to start one with the help of the clearing house. This clearing house which is faced with the problem of linking people over a wide geographical area also demonstrates the variety of alternatives to face-to-face meetings which have been made possible by computer technology. The linking of terminally ill and bedridden cancer patients through a computer network is one example.

And so support centres are beginning to accept that the 'classic' model of the spontaneous, self-directed, face-to-face self help group may not always be appropriate or adequate. It is likely that imaginative new strategies for facilitating mutual support outside this model will continue to be developed. Such strategies would imply continuing acceptance of the principle that mutual support is best organized around a common problem. But, of course, self help is often practised by people whose individual problems are very different but who have a common point of contact such as sharing a social activity or a cultural identity. Black self help seems to have this character. Supporting self help in this looser and less organized sense poses real difficulties for a support centre which has defined its own role according to the needs of discrete, identifiable, organized self help groups. If it moves outside this constituency it risks losing its identity and sense of purpose. The best solution may be to form alliances with those who are in a position to recognize and encourage the growth of self help activities in clubs and community organizations. The skills of supporting self help could then be multiplied in a variety of settings without diluting the support centre's own more precisely focused approach.

CONTRADICTIONS OF AN ENABLING APPROACH

Most support workers would subscribe to the view that their function is to help groups to realize their own aims and not to seek to interpret or redefine those aims even if they appear inappropriate or unsympathetic. A consequence of this view is that support should be equally available to all groups according to need.

Observation of work within a local support centre suggests that while there may be a strong general commitment to an enabling and equitable approach towards groups, a process of rationing none the less exists. Workers' personal values, commitments and assessments may be significant elements in the rationing process. Moreover, the level of help given to any one group may be determined more by the resources available within the support centre at that time than by an independent assessment of the group's needs. The danger is that rationing happens without outside scrutiny and some of the reason for inequities in levels of support will be hidden from groups.

A group designed for the support of people with disabilities became, in the view of the Self Help Team workers, over-dominated by enthusiastic, able-bodied professionals, thus compromising its self help status. A group for sufferers from a chronic disease seemed to be heavily influenced by the evangelical Christian principles of its founder and doubts arose about its openness to sufferers who did not share his beliefs. Although the Team made no attempt to intervene, its ambivalence was expressed by distancing itself from these groups and limiting its commitment of resources to them. The reasons for this stance were, however, not explained to the groups themselves.

Support workers may be fearful that any support they offer will be seen as an endorsement of a group's aims and activities. This can be a particularly difficult issue when a support centre is providing a public platform for groups. The compilation of a local self help directory is a good example. To include groups which offer little mutual support or which are poorly run is to risk misleading members of the public or professional workers who may refer new members. This could in the end reflect upon the judgement and competence of the support centre and undermine the value of the directory. It must be recognized too that groups evolve and change, often very rapidly. What begins as an informal group for mutual support and sharing may be taken over by a commitment to service-giving or fundraising. Is it still a self-help group and should it be acknowledged as such in a directory and actively supported in other ways?

When it encountered such dilemmas, the Self Help Team usually chose to give 'borderline' groups the benefit of the doubt, recognizing that a decision to exclude them from support and publicity would imply a controlling, standard-setting role, contradicting its enabling approach. None the less, it experienced a real tension between the tasks of being an honest ambassador for self help within the wider community and acting as a resource for groups. Beyond this was perhaps a further tension between a need to patrol its own boundaries as a self help support project and a desire to maintain links with groups who had moved away from a primary focus upon self help.

Another kind of difficulty arises when a support centre is invited to advise upon the running of an established group. The enabling ideal implies that there is a consensus within a self help group about its values, aims and structure. In practice, support workers may be invited to align themselves with members' competing interpretations of what the group is about. The Self Help Team was occasionally asked to perform a trouble-shooting role when a group, in the view of some members, was failing to work productively. Straightforward differences of opinion about an aspect of group management might be resolved by informed discussion but difficulties stemming from deeper personality conflicts were less susceptible to outside help. The Team was able to offer a sympathetic ear to disgruntled refugees from such groups but positive support of a particular faction was avoided. Maintaining a judicious distance from groups' internal problems was felt to be necessary to the Team's credibility and yet it could be very painful to witness a promising group collapse under the weight of personal disagreements.

THE AMBIVALENCE OF A PROTECTIVE ROLE

Many self help groups have a good and constructive relationship with a professional worker who is willing to act as a resource without seeking to dominate. Similarly, some local groups may gain helpful advice and practical resources from an affiliation to a national organization. But the Self Help Team has occasionally been called upon to support groups which have encountered local professionals and national bodies with less helpful attitudes. A support centre can offer a refuge and a breathing space for group leaders who are experiencing pressures from outside the group to proceed in particular directions. The function of an 'honest broker' between competing interests is clearly an important one.

It is, however, a function which needs to be exercised with caution and restraint. Consistent efforts to protect groups from powerful pressures could be seen as paternalistic. And to take on an openly campaigning role on general policy issues (e.g. hospital closures) relevant to self help groups could involve a risk of being dismissed as partisan and 'political' by statutory service agencies. This could undermine the support centre's credibility and diminish its effectiveness in promoting and explaining self help to professional workers. At the same time, support workers will be aware that the interests of self help groups and professional service providers usually diverge and often collide. Since their first commitment will be to the well-being of groups, few will stand back from offering advice about how to apply pressure upon statutory services in order to produce desired changes.

There is perhaps an important difference between a support centre's role in enabling groups to pursue their special concerns and a strategy of lobbying on behalf of all local groups. Both activities could be seen as a form of campaigning but raise different questions about the authority of the support centre. A support centre which works with groups on a one-to-one basis to plan a course of action is responding to their directly expressed needs. If, however, it mounts a more broadly based campaign, questions may be asked about whether it is legitimately representing self help groups in its area. There has been little discussion so far in England about whether a local support centre should be directly accountable to its self help constituency or about what structures would be needed to bring this about. It is sometimes argued that most self help groups are conservative and isolationist and would be reluctant to participate in a politically active forum. Undoubtedly, many groups would resist the development of representative structures. Self help may, however, be impelled to find an independent and authentic voice if it finds itself repeatedly hijacked by professional and political groups who wish to write their own versions of its aims.

In the meantime, local clearing houses will probably continue to tread a fine line between taking action at the specific request of groups to protect and promote their separate interests and assuming a broader and more controversial role as guardian and promoter of local self help.

THE COSTS OF ENCOURAGING INDEPENDENCE

The early development of most new self help groups is dominated by simple practical needs - finding a room, producing an information leaflet, paying for refreshments, and so forth. The preferred response of the Self Help Team has been to inform new group leaders about the facilities available within other local agencies and to show them how to use these facilities in order to find the right resources for their groups. The notion of creating an all-embracing self help resource centre has been resisted, although the Team does have a package of practical resources to draw upon at its discretion in its work with new groups. The arguments for this approach are sound. The direct provision of practical help is expensive both in money and time for a small organization; it would also expose a self help support centre to the temptation of 'colonizing' local self help groups, creating dependent attitudes and inhibiting their links with other agencies.

The Self Help Team has a local setting which makes this strategy particularly effective. It is based within a well-developed local resource and development agency whose various projects can provide many different kinds of practical help to new groups. In her paper, Judy Wilson has highlighted the particular significance of the agency's community radio project in providing groups with sympathetic and easy access to radio publicity. The up-to-date directory of premises offering meeting space within the city has been heavily used by self help groups. The host agency has lively contacts with a wide range of other statutory and voluntary organizations, providing the Self Help Team with a ready-made network.

Working through a local network is undoubtedly an effective means of mobilizing wider support for self help. None the less, as suggested earlier, it is a network which is particularly relevant to white groups with access to city centre facilities. It must be remembered too that some support centres will be set up in areas with a poor tradition of community development and may themselves be unsupported and isolated. They could find themselves with sole responsibility for providing groups with access to resources and little confidence to shift the priorities of other agencies towards supporting self help. The immediate cost of encouraging groups towards independence in such a situation could be very high, leaving them without the quantity and quality of practical help which they need to survive.

Over the long term the independence of self help groups can best be sustained by creating a more sympathetic and welcoming environment. Helmut Breitkopf has looked at the different roles that might be played by a variety of professional groups and institutions in supporting self help, thus complementing the specialized function of the self help support centre. It is clear that much of this potential remains untapped both in England and in Germany. Some support centres have worked to educate other agencies, particularly health and social welfare authorities, about the value of self help and have tried to persuade them to release some of their own resources for its support. But so far the support centre's role of self help educator has been eclipsed by its direct provision of support to self help groups. The Nottingham research suggested that while local health care workers were well informed about local self help, they had not taken on board the message that they had a vital part to play in supporting it. Unless an awareness of the support needs of self help groups is spread more widely within the community, particularly among professional groups, many groups will not find the help they need to begin and to survive. This may require local support centres to give rather less attention to developing their own direct links with groups and rather more to teaching other local agencies about self help support.

Support workers may, however, resist such a reordering of their priorities. The Nottingham research suggested that the direct support of new groups was seen by the Self Help Team staff as the most rewarding and successful element of their work. Its aims were precise, the outcomes were tangible and the rewards were considerable. In contrast, the provision of resources to established groups (who had mostly drifted out of regular direct contact with the Team) and the promotion of self help among the major statutory services had a speculative and perhaps rather erratic appearance. The workers lacked the clear goals and immediate feedback which their work with new groups provided.

A CONCLUDING NOTE

A great deal has been learned about the art of supporting self help through the work of support centres in England, West Germany and other countries. Certain guiding principles have emerged and have gained general acceptance. This does not mean that the practice of supporting self help has ceased to evolve. This paper has argued that support centres will encounter a number of tensions and contradictions as they try to incorporate agreed principles into their day-to-day tasks. These contain the seeds of further change.

In particular, self help support centres may need to question the relevance of the 'traditional' self help group to many sections of the community and, consequently, to encourage and support new mechanisms for enabling self help to happen. At the same time, they will want to preserve their own carefully developed role as a resource for self help, related to but distinct from general community development work. As self help inevitably becomes more diverse and fluid, support centres will continue to be vexed by the question of how far to extend their active support among local groups. Patrolling their own boundaries is likely to become increasingly difficult and contentious. They may be faced with demands to become more accountable to their self help constituencies, resulting in management structures which give groups a controlling voice in overall policy. The future direction of self help support work is, of course, a matter for speculation. There seems to be a strong rationale for support centres to focus more clearly upon developing good practice in self help support, undertaking some direct work with local groups but functioning primarily as a learning resource for other agencies engaged in developing self help. In order for this to happen, self help support workers would need to divert some attention from their rewarding contacts with new groups towards long-term promotional and co-ordinating tasks with uncertain outcomes. More fundamentally, a commitment would be needed from the statutory health and social welfare services to take on more responsibility for providing self help groups with consistent support. At present there is little evidence of such a commitment.

NOTES

1.   For a discussion of the rationale for self help support and its key organizing principles as defined by an experienced international group of support workers, see Supporting Self Help, Report on a Workshop, Leuven, Belgium, January 1986. Published by the International Information Centre on Self Help and Health, E. van Evenstraat 2C, B-3000, Leuven, Belgium.

2.   The New Jersey Self-Help Clearinghouse has published many articles and discussion papers about its work. Of particular relevance to the issue of computer applications for self help support work is: Edward J. Madara, 'The Self-Help Clearinghouse Operation: Tapping the Resource Development Potential of I&R Services'. New Jersey Self-Help Clearinghouse, Saint Clare's Hospital, Denvill, New Jersey 07834.

CONCLUDING NOTES

Stephen Humble

Shortly after the final meeting of our Anglo German research group, an article on a particular self help group called Victim appeared in a UK national newspaper. Here is an extract:

> Every Friday Tracy McCaig, 17, and her friend Paula O'Toole went to a local disco, the Tropicana Club in Deansgate, Manchester. They always followed their parents' instructions to telephone Peter Clare, a taxi driver known to them, to pick them up from the club in the early hours and then to telephone their parents to say they were on their way home.
>
> On the morning of Saturday, August 16, just as Paula was ringing her mother to say they were leaving the club, a police patrol vehicle had already begun its pursuit of a suspected stolen car, an Opel, in Whitefield, five miles from the Tropicana. By the time the cars reached Deansgate, one of Manchester's main roads and still busy in the early hours of Saturday morning, they had driven through three sets of red lights and were reaching speeds of 80 mph.
>
> The girls were already in the taxi and Mr Clare was driving at normal speed across Deansgate into Quay Street towards Paula's home in Salford, where Tracy would be spending the night. The Opel smashed straight into the taxi's side. Within minutes of Paula's call home, Tracy was dead and both Paula and Mr Clare were critically injured. The 18 year-old driver of the Opel and his 16 year-old passenger escaped with minor injuries. (The Guardian)

As a result of this terrible experience, Tracy's grandfather was motivated to join Victim, an organization formed some months before to support the relatives of victims of high speed police car chases and to campaign. Victim now has 48 families in contact with its original founder, Mrs Josie Taylor, herself the mother of a 20 year-old girl who, as a bystander, was killed as a result of a high speed police car chase.

First and foremost, of course, our sympathy goes out to bereaved relatives caught up in circumstances such as these, and we would want to wish success in Victim's campaign. But secondly, what does the formation of Victim tell us about the question of self help groups? Here are just some of a list of possible lessons:

> Victim is a self help group. It consists of people sharing a common problem who come together to try to help each other to do something about it.
>
> It is health and social services related. Whilst it is not so easily categorized as, say, a chronic disease self help group, which is clearly health related, it is concerned with supported bereaved people in a broader health sense.
>
> It has campaigning goals. It has pressure group attributes and campaigning may be its main activity. It may not so much seek to relieve bereavement as to reduce the risks in high speed police car chases.
>
> It may want to provide support for bereavement as well as campaigning, and it may switch from one to the other depending on the circumstances.
>
> It is highly specialized in the sense that these victims, though real enough for the relatives, are rare amongst the general population.
>
> It is not geographically localized. It may depend entirely on mailed letters and the telephone for its lines of communication.
>
> Finally, it was set up purely and simply through the exertions of a victim's relative. It was not stimulated through a voluntary, statutory or private organization. It may be said to have all the weaknesses of a new group struggling with statutory support and finance, or all the strengths of a group of committed members whose experience as bereaved relatives keeps them together in one common aim.

These possible lessons from the formation of Victim are speculative. But as a unique and recent example of self help, Victim usefully raises questions about aspects of self help groups which were discussed in the concluding meeting of our Anglo German groups. These aspects were as follows:

the definition and formation of self help groups
government policy on these groups
the role of the researcher in self help
Anglo German comparisons
the future of self help groups

We deal here with each of these aspects in turn.

As a group we concluded that the simple definition of 'people sharing the same problem and coming together to do something about it' served best. We agreed that too much time has been wasted in the past reformulating definitions of self help groups. We accepted that because of their diverse origins and structures and because they have different patterns of development, self help groups defy precise definition. Self help groups, for example, could be established by outsiders who did not share the problem common to the members. They could evolve into orthodox voluntary organizations with paid workers. They might be very local or more nationally based. They might meet in one place or simply communicate through newsletters or 'helplines' on the telephone system.

We were convinced that there had been a considerable growth in the formation of self help groups, certainly in the two countries we were addressing and probably throughout the industrialized world. None the less we accepted that there was a danger of exaggerating the growth of self help groups, in effect of seeing more in the phenomenon simply because we were looking for it.

This growth we attributed to general attitude change amongst the population at large, to a greater sense of empowerment amongst whole sections of society and a wide recognition of large gaps in welfare services.

There were also enabling factors, such as the growth of community development, and the development of specific self help support systems which have provided the resources and know-how enabling people to participate.

We thought, however, that a claim on the West German side that only 3% to 5% of the potential population were actively involved in self help groups probably applied to both countries. (We agreed that the proportion would be larger if all people passing through self help groups were considered.

The German data on Alcoholics Anonymous showed that AA reached some 8% of people affected with alcohol problems).
In acknowledging that only a small minority of people feel able and willing to join self help groups, still less to initiate them, we nevertheless recognized that some people, particularly disadvantaged people, do not presently have the opportunity to engage in self help. This might not be so true for the physically disadvantaged but we were agreed that poor people were not getting full opportunity of access. On the English side we were also concerned about lack of opportunity of access for ethnic minorities and on the West German side, for immigrant 'guest workers'.
We did not think that we could be more specific about the association between the growth in self help groups and general attitudes in favour of empowerment. We rejected the thesis too that concern over the financial costs of the welfare state itself caused self help groups to flourish. It might cross people's minds that ever greater expenditure on health had not brought about universal cures; and it was true that people were more suspicious about the capacity of the medical profession to treat health problems. But greater public expenditure on health and welfare was not thought to be the central explanatory feature of the growth of self help. There was no sense that self help groups had arisen specifically out of opposition to the dominance of the increasingly costly medical system. We were more certain that people were increasingly suspicious about the capacity of the medical profession to treat health problems and to deal with patients sufficiently sensitively. There was greater suspicion at large about purely 'medical' cures, and this had prompted some people to do something about it in a self help way.
On government policy we had as a group to confess that we were in a quandary about suggesting improvements to policy on supporting self help groups. We were keenly aware that more government resources for self help does not inevitably equal better government policy. On the contrary, increased funding and inappropriate funding could lead to the colonization of groups by the state, a by now well-established problem in statutory-voluntary relations. And many groups do not seek and do not want funds other than what their own members raise.
We gave a cautious welcome to the English model of the Self Help Alliance whereby government recognized the need to give cash to an alliance of national voluntary

organizations for the setting up of experimental, local networks of support to self help groups. This was welcomed because it took direct control out of government hands and into the voluntary sector. Our caution was due to our feeling that experimentation of the Alliance kind does not release government from its obligation to provide further support. The Self Help Alliance and the earlier research and development projects financed by the West German governments are a means to stimulate local government and other local statutory agencies to provide resources. The two governments' efforts at experimentation deserve applause. But the experimentation will lead to further demand on resources, by no means all of which can be met locally.

We were more sanguine about government health policy more generally in both countries. There was a feeling that both governments were keenly aware that general health policy could no longer be made without reference to the growth of lay health care in a general sense, and that this provided fertile soil for self help groups to flourish.

For a research group with vested interests in promoting research we were surprisingly as wary about research on self help groups as about government policy on them. Precisely because self help groups are about 'people doing their own thing' so this presents awkward dilemmas when assessing the making of policy on them or researching them. Too much policy, too much research, or policy and research of the wrong kind can do a great deal of damage.

There was a general feeling on our part that large-scale research was no longer appropriate. There is a good basis of knowledge now in both countries of the dimensions of self help, where it takes place, who participates and what the aims of groups are. We would want to support smaller scale, evaluative research of a kind which helps groups to clarify their own way of work so that they can work better. We were admittedly not very specific about what we meant here. But generally we wanted to shift from research outside groups to research alongside groups. This would be one-to-one consultancy-type research. This kind of research in turn poses a number of problems, not least the problem of funding. Most groups simply could not afford it. One way ahead would be for central and local government to ensure that where funds for the development of self help groups are given, a small proportion is allocated for evaluation purposes. It should be up to groups to decide on the kind of evaluation undertaken. The encouragement by government -

and by the independent foundations for that matter - of the formation of associations of social science researchers able to offer research and consultancy services would also assist.

We were struck by the convergence of self help between the two countries in terms of Anglo/German comparison. There were many times in our three meetings when we dwelt not on differences but on the similarities between England and West Germany. We accepted that there was convergence in terms of the following:

general attitude change in both societies in favour of self help

similar patterns in the growth and formation of self help groups

similar rates of participation in self help groups

similar policy problems in financing health and welfare services

a disturbing similarity in government perception that encouraging self help might help arrest health and welfare expenditure.

There were some matters of difference between the two countries which we noted. In particular, there seemed to be a traditional reluctance in West Germany to encourage state provision without evidence of the failure of informal and voluntary systems to provide. (This was due to the operating principle there of Subsidiarität - whereby the individual is expected to provide for him/herself, failing that his/her family and so on up the ladder until the state finally accepts responsibility.)

There seemed to be greater grassroots alliances of self help groups in West Germany, which is partly to do with various alliances between self help groups and a nationally based alternative movement. On the English side we need to find ways of encouraging alliances between groups where groups want to form alliances.

We also felt that there had been research and development work in a larger number of localities in West Germany than in England. We concluded though that the momentum for research and development had now switched from West Germany to England with the funding of the Self Help Alliance and its evaluation.

Finally, on the question of the future of self help we wondered whether it was a matter of what will happen or what we would like to see happen. We considered that the subject of self help was moving into mainstream public policy. It was not moving mountains and there was certainly no significant shift of attitude across the professional health and welfare spectrum. But government rhetoric had changed.

We expected to see continued growth in the points at which people are encouraged into self help. For example, more general practitioners would provide encouragement (though one or two in our group disagreed). There would be more local support centres and clearing houses. Community radio and television would provide more publicity. The impact of AIDS would and should lead to the formation of new self help groups.

But - and this is an important qualification - we accepted that there was a limit to people's interest in joining self help groups. (This was particularly shown by general evidence made available to our group about low levels of joining and particular evidence of low levels of joining in the case of parents with mentally handicapped children.) There is, as a consequence, a limit on the extent to which self help groups are able to go beyond servicing their own members' immediate needs and exert pressure on government, either singly or in combination.

Above all, we felt conscious of the need not to overclaim for what self help groups can achieve. There was a shift taking place in both countries from a medical or professional health and welfare model to lay-oriented care. The shift was gradual and self help groups played a part in bringing it about. No more could or should be claimed. It was a mood of realism that as a research group we wanted to inject.

BIBLIOGRAPHICAL REFERENCES

CHAPTER ONE

Some Remarks on West Germany's Health and Welfare System and the Position of Self Help

Jürgen Matzat

Branckaerts, J. and C. Deneke, 'Mutual Aid: From Research to Supportive Policy' - Report from a WHO Workshop in: Hatch, S. and I. Kickbusch (eds) 'Self Help and Health in Europe', World Health Organization, Copenhagen (1984), pp. 186-91

Deneke, C. 'Self Help Groups in Health' in Gordon, P. (ed.) 'Professionals and Volunteers: Partners or Rivals', King's Fund Publishing Office, London (1982), pp. 25-9

Flamm, F. (1983) 'The Social System and Welfare Work in the Federal Republic of Germany. Publications of the Deutscher Verein für öffentliche und private Fürsorge Frankfurt (2nd English edition)

Matzat, J. 'Zum Umgang mit der Selbsthilfebewegung (How to Deal with the Self Help Movement' in Anneken R. and T. Heyden (eds) Wege zur Veränderung: Beratung und Selbsthilfe (Ways to Change: Counselling and Self Help) Deutsche Gesellschaft für Verhaltenstherapie (German Association for Behaviour Therapy) Tübingen (1985) pp. 103-108

Matzat, J. 'Self Help Groups in West Germany. Developments of the Last Decade.

Bibliographical References

CHAPTER TWO

Government Policy on Self Help Groups in England

Stephen Humble

Brenton, M. (1985) 'The Voluntary Sector in British Social
    Services', Longman
Davies, B. (1977) 'Community Health and Social Services',
    Hodder and Stoughton
Gosden, P.H.J.H. (1973) 'Self Help', Batsford
Hallett, C. (1982) 'The Personal Social Services in Local
    Government'. Allen and Unwin
Humble, S. (1985) 'Charity Statistics 1984-5', Charities Aid
    Foundation
NAHA, NHS Handbook (1985) National Association of
    Health Authorities
Klein, R. (1983) 'The Politics of the National Health
    Service', Longman
Nissell, M. et al. (1980) 'The Welfare State', PSI
Richardson, A. and M. Goodman (1983) 'Self Help and Social
    Care', PSI

CHAPTER FOUR

The Development of Self Help Organizations: Dilemmas and
Ambiguities

Tina Posner

Hatch, S. and Hinton, T. (1986) 'Self Help in Practice: a
    Study of Contact a Family, Community Work and
    Family Support', Joint Unit for Social Services
    Research, University of Sheffield
Katz, A.E. and E. Bender (1976) 'The Strength in US' New
    Viewpoints, New York
Killilea, M. (1976) 'Mutual Help Organizations:
    Interpretations in the Literature' in: Caplan, G. and
    Killilea, M. (eds) 'Support Systems and Mutual Help:
    Multidisciplinary Explorations,' Greene and Stratton
Knight, B. and R. Hayes (1981) 'Self Help in the Inner City',
    London Voluntary Service Council, London
Mitchell, J. (1982) 'Looking After Ourselves: an Individual
    Responsibility?', Royal Society of Health Journal, 4, pp.

169-73

Richardson, A. and M. Goodman (1983) 'Self Help and Social Care: Mutual Aid Organizations in Practice', Policy Studies Institute, London

CHAPTER SIX

Why We Need Data

Dieter Grunow

Forschung u. Entwicklung im Dienst der Gesundheit. Programm der Bundesregierung. BMFT. Bonn. 1983

Freeman, H.E. and M.A. Solomon. The Future of Evaluation Research: An International Perspective. Paper from the 10th World Congress of Sociology, Mexico City. 1982

Glaser, B.G. Theoretical Sensitivity. Mill Valley, Cal. 1978

Grunow, D. et al. Gesundheitsselbsthilfe im Alltag. Stuttgart, 1983. Gesundheitsselbsthilfe durch Laien. Bielefeld. 1984

Halves, E. et al. Handlungsfelder und Entwicklungen von Selbsthilfegruppen. In Kaufmann (ed.) Staat, Intermediare Instanzen und Selbsthilfe. Munich. 1987

McKeown, 'The Role of Medicine. Dream, Mirage or Nemesis?' London. 1979

Rossi, P.H. and H.E. Freeman, 'Evaluation. A Systematic Approach'. Beverley Hills. 1985

Sechrest, L. Evaluating Health Care. In: Americ. Beh. Scientist 28 (1985), pp. 527-42

Senftleben, Die Qualität arztlicher Verrichtungen im ambulanten Versorgungsbereich. Munich. 1980

Stufflebeam, D.L. 'Meta-Evaluation. An Overview. In: Eval. Hlth. Prof. 1 (1978), pp. 17-43

INDEX